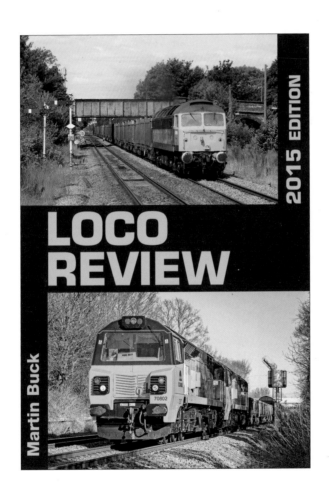

LOCO REVIEW

2015 EDITION

Martin Buck

FREIGHTMASTER

PUBLISHING

Contents

ISBN : 978-0-9558275-9-4

Published, November 2014 :

Freightmaster Publishing
158 Overbrook
SWINDON
SN3 6AY

www.freightmasterpublishing.co.uk

Printed By :

Stephens & George
Goat Mill Road
Dowlais
MERTHYR TYDFIL
CF48 3TD

www.stephensandgeorge.co.uk

Cover Images : Neil Harvey (top) / David Hayes (bottom)
Opposite   : Simon Howard

Note : All dates in the text are 2014, unless otherwise stated.

Setting the Scene

Welcome to *Loco Review 2015* and to begin with, a quote from a contributor:

"If someone had told me I'd be photographing a freight hauled by a two-tone green Class 47 in 2014, I wouldn't have believed them!"

Well, this is precisely what's been happening; GBRf spicing up proceedings by hiring Class 47s from Riviera Trains to haul scheduled WTT trains, notably gypsum and industrial sand. This nicely sets the scene with plenty of action involving Class 20s, 37s, 56s, especially on departmental services and that's not all; freight operators have also been busy complementing their loco fleets to make sure they have sufficient traction to fulfill their commitments, particularly:

Colas :

2 Class 37s resurrected.

20 Class 60s acquired from DBS.
60087, the first to enter service.

10 new Class 70s.

DRS :

25 new Class 68s.

These are working intermodal and ballast trains, whilst some are destined for Chiltern Railways, to replace Class 67s on the London Marylebone - Birmingham route.

GBRf :

21 low emission Class 66/7s.

Class 59/0 No.**59003 'Yeoman Highlander'** returns to the UK, after being exported to Germany 17 years ago to work stone trains on behalf of Yeoman / Deutsche Bahn, before moving on to Heavy Haul Power International.

Author's Gallery is a new addition. During compilation, 1,000s of images are viewed in order to pick the best ones to illustrate the featured stories and there is always some which fall outside this criteria and cannot be included. I have decided to reproduce a small number of these excellent images for you.

The Next Issue of *'Loco Review'* is already being planned, which should be equally as interesting as the current issue and will, I hope, be eagerly anticipated with much to look forward to. To whet your appetite, there will be Colas 37s, GBRf's new toy (No.59003), DRS Class 88 electric locos and a special portfolio celebrating the 125th Anniversary of the Forth Rail Bridge.

So, please turn the page and see for yourself how much there is to enjoy with locos, past and present, helping to make the railways that much more interesting. Enjoy.

Martin Buck

Background

On 7th January, GBRf announce that a contract with Sibelco Europe has been gained to provide freight services for its silica sand product. Silica sand will be transported from Sibelco's quarry in Kings Lynn, Norfolk, to Guardian Industries' UK glass making plant in Goole, Yorkshire, and Ardagh Group's UK glass sites in Barnsley and Doncaster. Two trains will run three days per week and one train two days per week to these locations.

Previously, DBS had the responsibility of moving sand from a loading terminal at Middleton Towers to the three plants using WBB branded 2-axle 'PAA' Sand Hoppers built by W H Davis between 1981 - 1983. The respective loaded train services are:

GBRf	6E84,	08:20 Middleton Towers - Barnby Dun	(MFO)
	6E84,	08:20 Middleton Towers - Monk Bretton	(TThO)
	6E88,	12:39 Middleton Towers - Goole Glassworks	(MWFO)

The Destinations

All three glass making plants are located in Yorkshire, served by either secondary railway routes or 'freight-only' lines:

Barnby Dun   : (Kirk Sandall) accessed off the South Yorkshire Joint Line.

Monk Bretton   : (Near Barnsley) located on a 'freight only' line, six miles from Oakenshaw South Junction (Wakefield). This is the remaining section of the former 'Midland Route' via Cudworth, the section from Swinton (Wath Road Junction) to Cudworth North Junction was closed in 1988 due to mining subsidence and has since been lifted.

Goole   : Accessed from Potters Grange Junction, a mile west of Goole station.

(Above) : 'PAA' 2-Axle Sand Hoppers, Nos. WBB 30021 & 30008 at Peterborough.   **Martin Buck**

(Opposite) : Just before 07:00hrs, on 21st April, the Barnby Dun train (6E83) is being loaded at Middleton Towers and there are still quite a few hoppers to load.   **Nick Slocombe**

66720 (left) leaves Downham Market on 18th April at 09:43hrs with 6E84 the 08:20 Middleton Towers - Barnby Dun loaded sand.

The King's Lynn branch is double track except for the sections between Littleport ByPass - Downham Market and Watlington - King's Lynn, where it is bi-directional single track.

66714 'Cromer Lifeboat' (top right) is seen after running round its train at King's Lynn, heading along the branch towards Middleton Towers and passing Hardwick Industrial Estate with 6L98 the 04:27 empties from Doncaster. Just above the tree line on the right, is the top of the Bentinck Dock grain silo.
Nick Slocombe (2?

66721 'Harry Beck' (bottom right) : Journey's end .... nearly six hours after leaving the loading terminal, No.66721 reverses 6E84, the 08:20 Middleton Towers - Barnby Dun loaded sand into the Ardagh (formerly Rockware) glassworks. **Alan Padley**

66709 'Sorrento' (above) passes the outskirts of Whittlesea on 16th April with a train of loaded sand 'Covhops', forming 6E88, the 12:39 Middleton Towers - Goole Glassworks. The Barnby Dun and Monk Bretton trains usually load to 28 wagons, both formed of the unique 'PAA' 2-Axle Sand Hoppers in the number range WBB 30001 - WBB 30060 (Design Code PA016A) and WBB 30101 - WBB 30112 (Design Code PA017A), built in the early 1990s by W H Davis at Langwith Junction, Shirebrook. **Nigel Gibbs**

Metronet

GBRf Sand : No.66722 "Sir Edward Watkin" (above) passes the site of Royston Junction with 6E84, the 08:20 Middleton Towers - Monk Bretton glassworks, on 8th April. Hard to believe that this was once a four-track main line!. **Neil Harvey**

GBRf Cars : On a glorious spring morning (1th March) No.66719 'METRO-LAND' (below) runs alongside the A702 at Wandel in the Upper Clyde Valley with 6X80, the 20:03 Southampton Western Docks - Mossend. **Alastair Blackwood**

In February, GBRf move into another new sector - *automotive* - and replace DB Schenker as traction provider for these services:

6X41	00:32	Dagenham - Garston	(MX)	GBRf 92
6X41	03:30	Dagenham - Garston	(MO)	GBRf 92
6L48	14:00	Garston - Dagenham	(SO)	GBRf 66

Two weeks later, GBRf gain a short term flow (six weeks) moving imported Renault cars from Southampton Western Docks to Scotland. The first flow begins on 10th March, viz:

6X80,	20:03	Southampton W. D.- Mossend	(MWO) GBRf 66

The wagons for the Anglo-Scottish flow are:

'IPAs'	: 87.4333.060-9	87.4333.031-0	87.4333.081-5	
	87.4375.038-8	87.4375.009-9	87.4375.033-9	87.4375.049-5
'IFAs'	: 87.4376.006-4	87.4376.009-8	87.4376.003-1	

Timings : 6X80

SOUTHAMPTON WESTERN DOCKS (20:03) - Southampton (20:19) - Eastleigh (20:31- 20:33)
Basingstoke (21:18) - Reading West Jct. (21:39) - Didcot East Jct. (21:56) - Oxford (22:12)
Banbury (22:41) - Leamington Spa (23:44)
Tyseley (00:12) - Landor Street Jct. (00:24) - Castle Bromwich Jct. (00:32) - Ryecroft Jct. (00:53)
Pleck Jct. (00:57) - Bushbury Jct. (01:12- 01:36) - Stafford (01:54-01:56) - Crewe (02:27)
Warrington Bank Quay (02:56) - Preston (03:58) - Carlisle (06:15) - Carlisle (06:33-07:45)
Beattock Summit (09:09) - Carstairs (10:19) - Law Jct. (10:45) - Holytown Jct. (10:53) - **MOSSEND (11:05)**

OK, another image depicting No.66719 on the first running of 6X80, Southampton Western Docks - Mossend, but why not? It's a beautiful day, in a beautiful part of the world. On 11th March, No.66719 (above) approaches Abington, 40 minutes late, slowing to enter Abington loops. **Keith McGovern**

6Z80

Not what one would normally expect to see coming along the West Coast Main Line at Cathiron (north of Rugby), a Network Rail Class 57/3 hauling a rake of car carriers. On 8th March, No.57306 (above), currently on hire to GBRf, heads south with 6Z80, Warrington Arpley - Tonbridge empty car carriers, destined for Southampton and the next loaded train of Renaults to Scotland. **Jamie Squibbs**

On 8th March, No.66719 takes over from No.57306 at Willesden (Acton lane Reception Sidings) for the remainder of 6Z80's journey to Tonbridge. With the light fading fast, No.66719 (below) is seen hauling the car carriers south at Dunton Green, which is between Orpington and Sevenoaks. **Alan Hazelden**

GBRf : On 14th April, the last rays of sunshine glint on 6L48, the 15:48 Garston - Dagenham, as Class 66/7 No.66730 'Whitemoor' (above) approaches Coton Lane road bridge, Tamworth.

The train is on an 11 mile section of the WCML between Tamworth and Armitage, which had been double track until modernisation saw it quadrupled, opening in September 2008.

John Whitehouse

DBS : DB Schenker gain an automotive flow in May. This involves moving imported Ford vehicles, sourced from the giant Ford plant in Genk (Belgium) and elsewhere in Europe, through the Port of Southampton to Garston, Merseyside. This is the first Ford traffic from Southampton West docks for a number of years; Freightliner had Ford automotive traffic some years ago, then the car terminal was left unused for about 3 years, prior to the Renault traffic starting in 2013.

6M66   09:32   Southampton Western Docks - Garston   (ThO)   DBS 66

No.66129 (below) passes a huge pile of scrap metal in Western docks, having left the car terminal a few minutes previously. It is running forward in order to run round by the Quay side. The traffic is solely Transit vans but other vehicles (Focus, C-Max and Ka) can also be conveyed. **Steve Stubbs**

HERITAGE TRACTION

GBRf 47/8 BH RIVIERA TRAINS ON HIRE VIA HNRC

GBRf, in lieu of new Class 66/7s, hire three Class 47/8s from Riviera Trains:

47812
47815 'Great Western'
47843 'Titan'

The first batch of 21 new GBRf Class 66 locos arrive by ship at Newport Docks, from USA, on 10th July.

The locos come from Electro-Motive Diesel (EMD) ahead of changes in EU emissions legislation which come into force from January 2015.

47812 (above) looks superb in two-tone green livery, as it approaches Gilberdyke station on 14th July with 4D94, the 10:21 Doncaster Roberts Road - Hull Coal Terminal empty gypsum.　　**Neil Harvey**

On a hot and sultry 31st July, the effect of loco exhaust and a heat haze, help to blur the approach of Nos.**47812** (D1916) + **47815 'Great Western'** (top right), as they 'clag' away from Hagg Lane, Gascoigne Wood, with 4D19, the 12:28 Drax - Doncaster Down Decoy loaded gypsum.

As well as imported gypsum, coal-burning power stations with flue gas desulfurisation produce large quantities of gypsum as a byproduct. It's used to make plasterboard and the British Gypsum factories at East Leake (Leics.), Kirkby Thore (Cumbria), Mountfield (East Sussex) and Sherburn-In-Elmet (Yorkshire) receive gypsum by rail.　　**Neil Harvey**

(Opposite) : "Giving it some Gyp" .... No.**47812** storms past the semaphore signals near Welton on 14th July with 4D95, the 15:00 Hull Coal Terminal - Doncaster Down Decoy imported gypsum.　　**Syd Young**

47815 'Great Western'

On 21st July, No.47815 (left) takes the Guardian glass factory line at Potters Grange Junction, Goole, with 6E88, 12:39 Middleton Towers - Goole Glassworks sand train.

Just as the sun was setting, the very last rays of light give a pink tint to the buildings in the background, especially noticeable on Goole's distinctive white 1927 built concrete water tower. **Martin Loader**

On 1st September, a pristine looking No.47815 (top right) passes through Thorne North with 4D95, the 12:16 Doncaster Down Decoy - Hull Coal Terminal gypsum empties, running 70 minutes late.

47815 (bottom right) passes Bentley on the Wakefield - South Elmsall - Doncaster main line on 7th July with 4D67, Wrenthorpe - Doncaster Decoy; the loco ran light to Wakefield earlier to pick up the rake of 'HYA' coal hoppers. **Alan Padley (2)**

GBRf seem to be finding plenty of work for these venerable old 47s. Away from gypsum and sand workings, On 2nd October, No.47815 'Great Western' (above) is allocated to work a special 6Z59, Immingham - Doncaster Hexthorpe Yard, a wagon move which is seen passing Kirk Sandall Junction. **Alan Padley**

On 30th May, 47843 'Vulcan' (above) reverses down the sidings into the glass works at Barnby Dun with 6E84 the 08:20hrs service from Middleton Towers. The two types of 2-axle 'PAA' sand hoppers are visible.

47812 + 47843 (below) get under way from a signal check at Knottingley on 8th August with 4D19, the 12:32 Drax - Doncaster gypsum, which are going via Knottingley - Milford Junction - Gascoigne Wood - Hambleton Junctions - Temple Hirst Junction and ECML to get to Doncaster. Apparently, 2 x Class 47s are too heavy to go round the curve between Knottingley East Junction and Knottingley South Junction, so cannot go via the direct route via Askern. Eggborough power station and Kellingley mine are also in view.

47843 'Vulcan' (above) makes its debut on 30th May and is seen crossing the River Dun Navigation on the fina
eg of the journey from Doncaster, working 6E84, the 08:20 Middleton Towers - Barnby Dun sand train
The train is approaching Kirk Sandall Junction.   **Alan Padley (3)**

47 FACT FILE

Number History :

47812	August 1989	ex - 47657	July 1986	47239	April 1974	D1916 November 1965
47815	August 1989	ex - 47660	September 1986	47155	February 1974	D1748 July 1964
47843	March 1990	ex - 47623	November 1984	47090	March 1974	D1676 April 1965

Names :

47812   Never named

47815   'GREAT WESTERN' : September 2005 at Crewe Works
         'Abertawe Landore' : July 2000 at Swansea High Street station

47843   'VULCAN'   : October 1965 at Cardiff Canton TMD

47815   January 1976 : A unique event in the history of a Class 47 loco.

As No.47155 at the time, allocated to Stratford TMD, this loco was hired to the CEGB Power Station at West Thurrock, Essex, to act as a temporary stationary generator, while a serious fault in one of the station's generator's field exciters was fixed. The buffers and bogies were removed and the loco was transported by road (on a Pickfords low-loader) to Thurrock, during 8th/9th January.

As it transpires, the main generator characteristics of a Class 47 matched that of the failed exciter. No.47155 did generate electricity in this role, not as a source of power to heat or light anything, simply to allow the power station generator to do so.

A withdrawn Class 45, No.45029, was in this role at Thorpe Marsh power station in 1982.

47812 : On 23rd June, in a rapidly fading but atmospheric light, Class 47/8s No.47812 + 47843 'Vulcan' (above) pass Hatfield Colliery and the site of the February 2013 landslip with loaded 'PAAs' in tow, forming 6E88, the 12:39 Middleton Towers - Goole sand. The time is 20:20hrs. **Alan Padley**

47843 'Vulcan': Unusually, routed through platform 3, No.47843 (above) opens up after a signal check and produces a good plume as it passes through Doncaster station on 11th July with 6E88, the 12:39 Middleton Towers – Goole. Great sight, great sound, although the passengers on the platform would probably disagree!   **Alan Padley**

Anglo-Scottish 'Bins' - the end of Roxby

Background

The GMC (Greater Manchester Council) refuse trains of containerised waste - 'Binliners' - have been running since 1981, eventually serving four Refuse Transfer Stations (RTS) at:

> Bredbury   Dean Lane   Northenden   Pendleton

The waste was originally offloaded at a former quarry landfill site at Appley Bridge, between Wigan and Southport, until being temporarily diverted to Wakefield. When Appley Bridge became full in 1993, the GMC trains switched to a landfill site in former ironstone workings at Roxby, near Scunthorpe.

Roxby Filling Up / Scottish 'Bins'

GMC switch to moving their waste to a new waste processing plant at Runcorn which will handle up to 850,000 tonnes of pre-treated waste (known as Refuse Derived Fuel or RDF) each year. This plant will generate up to 70MW of electricity and up to 51 MW of heat, all of which will be used by neighbouring chemicals manufacturer INEOS.

During this transition period, GMC use a landfill site at Oxwellmains in Scotland (used by the Edinburgh 'Binliners') to deposit domestic waste, initially from Bredbury RTS. The full service is operated by Freightliner Heavy Haul and runs as:

FHH	6E06, 09:32 Bredbury R.T.S. - York Yard	(MWFO)
	6S15, 15:46 York Yard - Oxwellmains	(MWFO)
	6M00, 09:58 Oxwellmains - Bredbury	(TThO)

However, Roxby is now full and the last GMC 'Binliners' run to Roxby in June.

6M00 : It takes two hours for the train to run some 58 miles from Oxwellmains to Millerhill and back in order for it to go south. The timings between these two points are:

Oxwellmains (10:05) - Oxwellmains Crossover (10:08) - Dunbar (10:10) - Drem (10:22) - Prestonpans (10:31) - Monktonhall Jct (10:39) - **Millerhill (10:47 / 11:12)** - Monktonhall Jct (11:22) - Prestonpans (11:26) - Drem (11:35) Drem U.P.L. (11:36 / 11:44) - Dunbar (11:59 / 12:01) - **Oxwellmains Crossover (12:05)**

6M00 is 30 minutes late on 25th February as it passes Ballencrieff with No.66510 (above) atop the Oxwellmains - Bredbury empty 'Bins', on its way to Millerhill. The large mound is North Berwick Law, a conical volcanic plug of hard phonolitic trachyte rock, which rises incongruously from the surrounding landscape. It overlooks the East Lothian town of North Berwick and is 613 ft above sea level.

(Opposite) : Having made its reversal, FHH Class 66/5 No.66514 is seen on 8th April, heading south past Markle level crossing (Milepost 22m 20chs), just under five miles east of Drem.

On a dismal 25th March, No.66514 (below) has just crossed over the 'Up Main' and joined the 'Down Main' after leaving the waste disposal terminal at Oxwellmains with the empty 'binliner' returning to Bredbury. The Blue Circle cement works dominates the background. **Keith McGovern (3)**

The 'Shanks' / 'Freightliner' branded Class 66/5 No.66522 (above) heads for Millerhill and a reversal on 22nd March, whilst working 6M00, the 09:58 Oxwellmains - Bredbury. The loco is passing Prora farm, near Drem, on the ECML, and 6M00 is running about 30 mins late at this point.

On 21st January, Class 66/5 No.66547 (below) sits in the 'Up Passenger' Loop at Drem with 6M00 empty 'Binliner' to allow 1E13, the 07:55 Inverness - London King's Cross to overtake. The HST set is headed by Class 43 power car No.43312. **Keith McGovern (2)**

End of the Road for the Trans-Pennine Roxby 'Binliners'

To mark the passing of 22 years of Trans Pennine GMC 'Binliners', running to Roxby, here's a few nostalgic momentos, both past and present ....

In amazing light, FHH Class 66/5 No.66522 (right) appears almost luminescent as it sweeps round the curve and into view, approaching Marsden on 16th January with the late-running 6M07, 11:09 Roxby - Pendleton empty 'Binliner'.

No.66522 was repainted in this unique FHH/Shanks colour scheme in November 2004 in conjunction with the flow of containerised domestic waste from Dagenham Dock to Calvert landfill site.

Neil Harvey

(Overleaf)

"Remember A Day Before Today" ....

.... when the likes of 47s, 56s and 60s were commonplace on the 'Bins'!

47018 (Page 26, top) in Railfreight Grey, Large Logo livery, heads west along the Calder Valley main line on 16th May 1988 at Dover Bridge, Eastwood, with 6M62, the 11:08 Wakefield Cobra - Northenden empty 'Binliner'. The train is passing Milepost 21miles and 60chains, which is the mileage from Manchester Victoria via Rochdale.

60045 'The Permanent Way Institution' (Page 26, bottom) is captured passing through Paddock Cutting, Huddersfield, on 11th May 2006 with 6M05, the 09:30 Roxby - Northenden empty 'binliner'. Freightliner Heavy Haul took over the GMC domestic waste trains from EWS (now DBS) in April 2008, leaving DBS with just the Edinburgh and Brentford / Northolt 'Binliners' in 2014.

60007 (Page 27, top) sporting the classic Loadhaul orange & black colours, passes Addingford Lane, Horbury, on 21st June 1999 with 6E06, the 09:40 Bredbury - Roxby loaded GMC containerised waste. The yard lights at Healey Mills can be seen in the distance and this was a time when the yard was relatively busy and where a 'Binliner' could change loco crew.

56127 (Page 27, bottom) in two-tone grey livery and sporting Transrail branding, is seen approaching the east end of Healey Mills Yard on 11th May 2001 with 6M07, the 10:45 Roxby - Pendleton empty 'bins'. This vantage point is Storrs Hill Road bridge, which leads off the A642 Wakefield - Huddersfield and has been a popular location among enthusiasts for many a long year.

Neil Harvey (4)

Sowerby Bridge : Class 47/3 No.47329 (above) passes through Sowerby Bridge on 14th June 1988 with 6M62, the 12:08 Wakefield Cobra - Northenden GMC empty 'Binliner'. Of note is the signal carried on a Lancashire and Yorkshire Railway right hand bracket, which was taken out of use in May 1985 when Sowerby Bridge West signal box closed along with Mytholmroyd West signal box. On the hillside stands Wainhouse Tower, built in the 19th century and standing at 253ft tall. It is one of the most prominent landmarks in Calderdale.   **Neil Harvey**

Slaithwaite : FHH Class 65/9 No.66597 'Viridor' (above) heads 6M05, the 09:30 Roxby - Northenden on 19th November 2013 across Crimble Viaduct, one of two viaducts at Slaithwaite. In October 2011, No.66957 'Viridor' was named at Viridor's recycling and resource recovery facility in Manchester. The Company is a recycling, renewable energy and waste management company and has a 25 year contract with the GMC.   **Derek Holmes**

'Binliner' Miscellany

Calvert Landfill Filling Up!

It's not only Roxby landfill site which is filling up, it's Calvert too, which is accessed via a single track of the former Great Central alignment through Quainton Road.

As a result of this, only the Cricklewood 'Binliner' still goes there, the Brentford and Northolt 'Binliners' have been combined and re-routed to Scunthorpe. There trainplan is:

DBS			
	0A01,	Acton Yard - Northolt R.T.S.	light engine
	6A01, 20:09	**Northolt R.T.S. - Southall Yard**	
	0A02,	Southall Yard - Brentford R.T.S.	light engine
	6A02, 22:29	**Brentford R.T.S. - Southall Yard**	
	6E02, 23:39	**Southall Yard - Scunthorpe F.D.**	
	6V04, 18:59	**Scunthorpe F.D. - Southall Yard**	
	6A04, 01:30	**Southall Yard - Brentford R.T.S.**	
	0A04,	Brentford R.T.S. - Southall Yard	light engine
	6A06, 05:10	**Southall Yard - Northolt R.T.S.**	
	0A06,	Northolt R.T.S. - Acton Yard	light engine

Just to muddy the picture, the Northenden - Runcorn 'binliner' becomes confusing when it is temporarily sent to Calvert RTS for discharge, w/c 7th July. The details are:

FHH			
	6F32, 04:54	**Northenden - Crewe**	(MWO)
	6Z22, 06:48	**Crewe - Calvert**	(MWO)*
	6M23, 19:20	**Calvert - Crewe**	(MWO)*
	6Z32, 04:10	**Crewe - Northenden R.T.S.**	(TThO)

* runs in the path of the Cricklewood - Calvert 'Binliner' between Acton Wells and Calvert.

66081 (above) is passing Hatfield & Stainforth on 13th July with 6V04, the 18:59 Scunthorpe F.D. - Southall Yard, empty Greater London 'Binliner'. The time is approaching 18:45hrs and the train is running 60 minutes early at this point in its journey. Shots of westbound freights taken on the north side of the line are a pleasing alternative to the more usual views associated with this location.   **Alan Padley**

66413

Ex-DRS Class 66/4 No.66413 (right) passes Hanch in the Trent Valley (WCML) on 7th July with 6Z22, the 06:48 Crewe Basford Hall - Calvert GMC loaded 'Binliner'; the first day this new flow ran. **John Whitehouse**

Meanwhile, 6Z22 (originating as 6F32, 04:54hrs Northenden - Crewe) is seen again, running 275 minutes late, as No.66413 (middle) heads over the crossover on the approach to Princes Risborough. **Geoff Plumb**

It's All Over .... After years of sending rubbish to Roxby Gullet, Scunthorpe, the last GMC loaded train was despatched in June and the empty containers returned to Pendleton RTS depot.

However, a few weeks later, a train of empty flats is despatched to collect some remaining containers at Roxby. These return to Northenden, in what proved to be the last 'Binliner' train from Roxby to Manchester ....

No.66413 (below) passes Ravensthorpe (Thornhill LNW Junction) with 6M05, Roxby - Northenden and is about to be overtaken by First Trans-Pennine Express Class 185 No.185140 on 1P43, 13:28 Middlesbrough - Manchester Airport. **Derek Holmes**

Background

After a long period of decline, freight traffic finally stops running to & from Thamesport container terminal on the Isle of Grain. This means that only aggregate trains (sand and stone) remain working on this freight only branch line.

The German carrier, Hapag-Lloyd moves its North America-Europe Gulf Atlantic Express (GAX) and Gulf Mexico Express (GMX) services, plus its Latin America/North America-Europe Pacific Atlantic Express (PAX) service to Southampton in October 2013. Previously, Hapag-Lloyd, along with partners Zim Line and Mitsui OSK Lines, had also stopped their Africa-Europe WAX/NAF/ARN service in July 2013; calling only at Antwerp and Hamburg in Europe instead. Evergreen also switch to Felixstowe.

Another factor contributing to the demise of Thamesport, was the opening of the London Gateway 'deep-sea' container port at Thurrock in November 2013, with the arrival of the MV. 'MOL Caledon', a 58,000-tonne container ship, laden with fruit and wine from South Africa.

Last train : 6th November 2013 : **4M49, 18:11 Thamesport - Lawley Street**

History

In 1990, Maritime Transport Services Ltd constructed a container port on the southern coastline of the Isle of Grain, taking over the area previously occupied by BP. In 1998, Thamesport was sold to Hutchison Ports (UK), who in turn sold it to Maritime Transport in 2001.

Thamesport lies some 11 miles at the end of a single line, which diverges from the North Kent main line, east of Gravesend, at Hoo Junction.

The line runs in an easterly direction across the Hoo Peninsula, passing near the villages of Cooling, High Halstow, Cliffe and Stoke before reaching the Isle of Grain and the container port on its eastern tip.

The latest loco class to visit the container terminal at Thamesport was Freightliner's 'Powerhaul' Class 70.

On 28th March 2013, a fully laden 4O88, Lawley Street - Thamesport 'liner is seen heading away from Dartford on the North Kent Line, as the driver of No.70008 (left) piles on the power.

In the background, on the other side of the bridge, a Class 465 'Networker' EMU is stabled in the 'Up' carriage Sidings at Dartford station.

Ian Cuthbertson

Comparison Timetables

November 2013

4O82, 23:49 Leeds - Thamesport	FHH 66	4E24, 10:39 Thamesport - Leeds
4O88, 06:24 Lawley Street - Thamesport	FHH 66	4M49, 18:11 Thamesport - Lawley Street
4O24, 11:00 Bristol - Thamesport	FHH 66	4V26, 12:00 Thamesport - Bristol
4O80, 21:02 Trafford Park - Thamesport	FHH 66	4M57, 21:10 Thamesport - Trafford Park

November 2003

4Z55, 06:50 Ditton - Thamesport	EWS 66	4Z26, 20:47 Thamesport - Ditton
4O80, 21:39 Trafford Park - Thamesport	FHH 66	4M57, 21:10 Thamesport - Trafford Park
4O87, 10:26 Tilbury - Thamesport	FHH 66	4L86, 10:39 Thamesport - Tilbury
4Z55, 20:24 Scunthorpe - Thamesport *	EWS 66	6E55, 18:35 Thamesport - Scunthorpe

* "Evergreen" containerised steel

Fastline : A new railfreight operator, part of Jarvis plc, briefly entered the intermodal market in May 2006 running a thrice-weekly container train from Doncaster Railport to Thamesport using a fleet of three refurbished Class 56 locos (Nos.56301 - 56303). This was followed later the same year by a service from Birch Coppice, the respective services being:

4O90, 11:01 Doncaster - Thamesport	FLine 56	4E90, 00:07 Thamesport - Doncaster
4O90, 13:36 Birch Coppice - Thamesport	FLine 56	4M90, 00:07 Thamesport - Birch Coppice

Due to poor loadings, these services were christened by railway enthusiasts the "Fresh Air Express" and, as you can imagine, did not run for long!

Portfolio

A small selection of images has been assembled to mark the passing of freightliner traffic to Thamesport, featuring Class 47, 56, 57, 66 and 70 traction.

Fastline used a fleet of three Class 56s to haul the intermodal services running between Thamesport and Birch Coppice, Nos.56301/2/3, all of which sported Fastline's striking livery. On 19th June 2006, the 4O90, 11:01 Doncaster Railport - Thamesport is seen headed by Class 56 No.56302 (above) approaching Wandsworth Road station with a 'heavy' load of four containers. **Nick Slocombe**

'47s'

On 21st March 1997, a shabby-looking Class 47/0 No.47204 (above) passes through Kensington Olympia wit
4O86, the 07:46 Crewe Basford Hall - Thamesport (Grain) freightliner. This particular loco was rebuilt as
Class 57 in April 2000, becoming No.57012.

On 16th June 1999, Class 47/0 No.47157 (below) accelerates past Hoo Junction with a well-loaded 4S56,13:4
Thamesport - Coatbridge. No.47157 was named 'Johnson Stevens Agencies' in December 1995 at Crewe TMD an
disposed of at C. F. Booth, Rotherham, in December 2004.   **Nick Slocombe (2**

No.47293 (above), allocated to the MDAT Pool (Railfreight Distribution, Tinsley) is seen working an unidentified Freightliner to Grain on 27th February 1992 at Dartford Junction, coming off the Sidcup line. The other line serves stations to Slade Green, Deptford and London Bridge. No.47293 was named 'Transfesa' at Tilbury in November 1997 and scrapped in July 2007 at EMR, Kingsbury.

Freightliner Two Tone Green Class 47/0 No.47114 'Freightlinerbulk' (below) is seen heading through Gravesend on 28th August 1999 working a 'liner to Grain. The loco was named at Thames Terminal, Purfleet, by Mike Gray, the terminal manager on 12th May 1997. The 'Freightliner' part of the name is in standard silver, the 'bulk' part in light green. No.47114 was disposed of in March 2005 at C. F. Booth, Rotherham.   **Ian Cuthbertson (2)**

The Grain Branch

Journey's end, or the beginning in this case, as Class 47/0 No.47206 'The Morris Dancer' (above) leaves Thamesport in 1st June 1999 with 4M96, the 19:37hrs service to Crewe Basford Hall. The train is passing Medway CCGT power station, operated by AES at the time. In September 2004, No.47206 became No.57605 and is still operational for First Great Western. **Nick Slocombe**

A panoramic view of the Grain branch is possible from the A228 road bridge, which spans the line at Stoke Marshes on the Isle of Grain. On 8th July 2013, Freightliner low emission Class 66/9 No.66955 passes Stoke Crossing with a fully-laden 4M49, 18:11 Thamesport - Lawley Street freightliner. **Richard A. Jones**

Class 57 No.57004 'Freightliner Quality' (above) arrives at Thamesport on 16th June 1999 with an overnight freightliner service, this being 4O88, the 23:41hrs from Leeds. Freightliner unveiled their new Class 57 locos in July 1998, a fleet of 12, all Class 47 rebuilds, but fitted with a General Motors 2,500hp engine. No.57001 was rebuilt from Class 47/3 No.47347 in March 1999.   **Nick Slocombe**

On 2nd July 2011, Class 66/5 No.66558 (below) passes under the A228 Stoke Bridge flyover with 4O24, the 11:00 Bristol - Thamesport empty 'wineliner'. A daily train brings imported wine to Bristol via Felixstowe (4V32), Thamesport (4V26), or Tilbury (4V30). The wine ends up at Constellation Europe's Avonmouth warehouse, which is the largest in Europe and holds a staggering 57 million bottles of wine.   **Ian Cuthbertson**

Background

The Channel Tunnel was one of Europe's biggest infrastructure projects. Work started in 1987 and took seven years to complete, at an astonishing cost of £9,000,000,000. The Tunnel is 31 miles long (24 miles under the sea) at an average depth of 150 feet under the seabed.

Opening

1st June 1994 : the first freight to pass through the Tunnel was a trainload of Rover cars bound for Milan, Italy, hauled by SNCF Class 222 locos, No.22379 + No.22403.

Motive Power

Initially, SNCF provide the traction from Dollands Moor to France and Railfreight Distribution (RfD) had responsibility of domestic train services between Wembley Yard and Dollands Moor, using a fleet of Class 47 locos, until the arrival of new Class 92s in January 2006.

Services

Initially, car trains, intermodal and wagonload services, followed later on by dedicated product trains, such as steel to Ebange and china clay slurry from Antwerp. However, hazardous materials (such as nuclear flasks) are prohibited from moving through the Tunnel.

All freight is staged at Dollands Moor freight yard; Frethun yard, Calais, on the other side. Despite more through services being introduced, problems have curtailed growth. The reasons for this include French train drivers going on strike, high access charges and security Issues with asylum seekers and migrant workers boarding trains to gain illegal entry into the UK.

Notable Train

Since the Channel Tunnel opened, the **'BLUE TRAIN'** has been ever-present.

This service runs between Dagenham (East London) and Silla (near Valencia, Spain), operated by Transfesa and carries motor parts in 'curtainsiders', on behalf of the Ford Motor Company.

A unique feature of the wagons used on this service (IFA'/'IFB' 4-Wheel Container Flats) is that they can change wheel base gauge, which is necessary for through running to and from Spain. This takes place at Portbou on the Franco/Spanish border, where there is a TALGO Automatic Track Gauge Changeover System facility.

DBS / HS1 : From November 2013, some services run via HS1 and the first is a new intermodal to Wroclaw, Poland. At 06:12hrs on 3rd July, with the Queen Elizabeth II road bridge visible behind, DBS Class 92 No.92041 'Vaughan Williams' (above) is on HS1, having just emerged from under the River Thames at West Thurrock with 6L21, the 22:03 Dollands Moor - Ripple Lane. **Stuart Chapman**

Wagonload services could be a variety of wagons. Class 47/0 No.47270 'Swift' (above) heads through Swanley on 12th May 1995 with a service for Wembley, which includes 'Cargowaggons', a single 'TIA' Bogie Tank and two 'JIA' Bogie Starch Tanks.   **Ian Cuthbertson**

Dollands Moor freight yard, near Folkestone in Kent, was purposely built in 1988 to handle Channel Tunnel freight. On 24th June 1998, Class 92 No.92028 'Saint Saens' (below) is seen leaving with 4M36, the 17:42 Dollands Moor - Wembley, having arrived earlier as 4215, the 12:43 service from Muizen. This image is taken from the top of Saltwood Tunnel as the train joins the South East main line.   **Nick Slocombe**

Dollands Moor : Spring 1996 : (Monday - Friday)   UK Internal Services

Time	Code	Train	Traction	Notes
08:00	6O58	02:11 Washwood Heath - Dollands Moor	Rfd 47s	to Lille
08:23	6M23	08:23 Dollands Moor - Wembley	Rfd 47s	from Evian
11:45	6O56	09:37 Wembley - Dollands Moor	Rfd 47s	to Lille
13:45	6M34	13:45 Dollands Moor - Wembley	Rfd 47s	from Somain
15:00	4O63	12:45 Wembley - Dollands Moor	Rfd 47s	to Valencia
17:20	4M35	17:20 Dollands Moor - Wembley	Rfd 47s	from Perpignon
17:42	4M36	17:42 Dollands Moor - Wembley	Rfd 47s	from Milan (Oleggio)
18:12	4M37	18:12 Dollands Moor - Wembley	Rfd 47s	from Milan (Melzo)
18:50	4M38	18:50 Dollands Moor - Wembley	Rfd 47s	from Bettembourg
19:15	4M39	19:15 Dollands Moor - Wembley	Rfd 47s	from Valencia
20:15	4M42	20:15 Dollands Moor - Wembley	Rfd 47s	from Novara
20:44	4M51	20:44 Dollands Moor - Wembley	Rfd 47s	from Milan (Pioltello)
21:15	4M52	21:15 Dollands Moor - Wembley	Rfd 47s	from Milan (Rogoredo)
21:20	6M66	21:20 Dollands Moor - Washwood Heath	Rfd 47s	from Arluno
21:20	6V66	21:20 Dollands Moor - Avonmouth	Rfd 47s	from Turin
22:00	4O70	19:49 Wembley - Dollands Moor	Rfd 47s	to Paris
22:15	4O71	19:20 Wembley - Dollands Moor	Rfd 47s	to Muizen
22:28	6M59	22:28 Dollands Moor - Wembley	Rfd 47s	from Genk
23:15	4M63	23:15 Dollands Moor - Wembley	Rfd 47s	from Milan (Rogoredo)
23:45	6M64	23:45 Dollands Moor - Wembley	Rfd 47s	from Evian
23:45	7X81	20:55 Wembley - Dollands Moor	Rfd 47s	to Silla / ex-Dagenham
00:50	6O77	22:36 Wembley - Dollands Moor	Rfd 47s	to Genk
01:40	6M13	01:40 Dollands Moor - Wembley	Rfd 47s	from Somain
02:00	6O95	16:33 Longbridge - Dollands Moor	Rfd 47s	to Arluno
02:15	4O46	00:07 Wembley - Dollands Moor	Rfd 47s	to Perpignon
03:00	6O67	00:53 Wembley - Dollands Moor	Rfd 47s	to Lille
03:12	4M16	03:12 Dollands Moor - Wembley	Rfd 47s	from Muizen
03:17	4M17	03:17 Dollands Moor - Wembley	Rfd 47s	from Paris
03:25	4O48	01:23 Wembley - Dollands Moor	Rfd 47s	to Milan (Melzo)
04:15	4O49	02:10 Wembley - Dollands Moor	Rfd 47s	to Milan (Rogoredo)
04:17	7X20	04:17 Dollands Moor - Wembley	Rfd 47s	from Silla / to Dagenham
04:35	4O50	02:28 Wembley - Dollands Moor	Rfd 47s	to Milan (Rogoredo)
05:10	4O51	03:02 Wembley - Dollands Moor	Rfd 47s	to Milan (Pioltello)
05:25	4O52	03:22 Wembley - Dollands Moor	Rfd 47s	to Novara
05:40	4O53	03:33 Wembley - Dollands Moor	Rfd 47s	to Milan (Oleggio)
06:10	4O55	04:10 Wembley - Dollands Moor	Rfd 47s	to Bettembourg

Codes : ▐ Automotive   ▐ 'Connectrail' (ie. Wagonload)   ▐ Intermodal

China Clay Slurry : In January 2008, a new service commences from Antwerp (Belgium) to Irvine in Scotland (replacing the long standing 6S55, Burngullow - Irvine), bringing in china clay slurry for use in the paper making industry. On 8th February 2013, Class 92 No.92016 (above) approaches Eynsford station with 6B45, the 12:13 (FO) Wembley - Dollands Moor empty slurry tanks. **Alan Hazelden**

47s in Pairs were a common sight until displaced by other traction, notably the Class 92s. On 1st March 1998, diversions were in place; intermodals sent via Tonbridge and Redhill; wagonload and cars via Sevenoaks. The trains were worked by pairs of 47s on this day (double-headed as insurance) and No.47049 'GEFCO' (opposite) leads a fellow Class 47 through Tonbridge with 4M31, the 12:14 Dollands Moor - Wembley intermodal. **Nick Slocombe**

Dollands Moor : Spring 2014 (Monday - Friday)

Departures

Code	Train		Traction	Commodity
6B20	06:46	Dollands Moor - Wembley	DBS 66	Bottled Water (ex-Evian)
4E26	07:45	Dollands Moor - Scunthorpe	DBS 92	Empty Steel (ex-Ebange)
6L21	22:03	Dollands Moor - Ripple Lane	DBS 92	Ford 'Blue Train' (ex-Silla)
4Q21	22:17	CT Boundary - Ripple Lane	DBS 92	Intermodal (ex-Wroclaw, Poland)
4M90	22:15	Calais Frethun - Daventry	GBRf 92	Intermodal (ex-Novara)
6M14	00:06	Dollands Moor - Ditton	DBS 66	Aluminium (ex-Neuss)
4L33	00:53	Dollands Moor - Ripple Lane	DBS 66	Intermodal (ex-Padova)
4M31	01:04	Dollands Moor - Hams Hall	DBS 66	Intermodal (from Domodossola)
6S94	03:05	Dollands Moor - Irvine	DBS 92	China Clay Slurry (ex-Antwerp)

Arrivals

Code	Train		Traction	Commodity
6B45	12:13	Wembley - Dollands Moor	DBS 92	Empty China Clay (to Antwerp)
4B45	12:31	Wembley - Dollands Moor	DBS 67s + 92	Intermodal
6O32	09:59	Margam - Dollands Moor	DBS 66	Steel
4O57	15:36	Hams Hall - Dollands Moor	DBS 92	Intermodal (to Domodossola)
6D71	20:04	Wembley - Dollands Moor	DBS 92	Wagonload
4O26	14:22	Scunthorpe - Dollands Moor	DBS 92	Steel (to Ebange)
4O93	21:25	Daventry - Dollands Moor	GBRf 92	Intermodal (to Novara)
6O23	22:22	Ripple Lane - Dollands Moor	DBS 92	Ford 'Blue Train' (to Silla)
6O16	20:11	Ditton - Dollands Moor	DBS 66	Empty Cargowaggons (to Neuss)
4Q20	23:36	Ripple Lane - Dollands Moor	DBS 92	Intermodal (to Wroclaw, Poland)

ERPS Class 37/6s

In November 1994, Eurostar services began running between London Waterloo International, Gare du Nord (Paris) and Brussels South. ERPS Class 37/6 locos could be seen towing Eurostar sets (ECS) between North Pole depot, Waterloo and Dollands Moor. On 26th June 1995, Nos.37609 + 37604 (above) were seen towing a Eurostar set to Dollands Moor through Shortlands Station.

Automotive

No.47365 'Diamond Jubilee' (above) is seen in a pretty shabby looking state (February 1998) entering Wandsworth Road station with 6O95, the 09:52 Washwood Heath - Dollands Moor, conveying Rover vehicles to Italy. This loco was named at ICI Wilton in September 1986 and scrapped in October 2007.   **Ian Cuthbertson (2)**

Intermodal

DBS : It's common practice for DBS to send Class 67s to Dollands Moor for fuelling, usually tucked inside behind a Class 92, on 4B45, the 12:31 (MO) Wembley - Dollands Moor intermodal. On 30th September 2013, No.67019 + 67006 'Royal Sovereign' (above) are on their own, double-heading 4B45, as the power is applied up the bank from Otford towards Kemsing.

GBRf : A colourful combination; 'Rainbow Warrior' Class 66/7 No.66720 + Class 92 No.92032 (below) approach Fen Pond Lane road bridge, Ightam, on 16th December 2011 with a late 4L06, 21:30 Dollands Moor - Ripple Lane. This service carries fruit from Spain in refrigerated containers.   **Alan Hazelden (2)**

Transfesa 'Blue Train'

On Monday, 17th May 2010, Cola Class 66/4 No.66845 (top left) still in DRS livery, approache Upper Holloway station with 7L23, the 04:17 Dollands Moor Dagenham.

The train is seen passing the 'portacabin' type signal box which opened in 1985 to replace two older Midland Railway signa boxes.

The wagons used on the 'Blu Train' are 'IFA'/'IFB' 4-Whee Container Flats, numbered:

(French) : 71. 4438. 001 to 070
(Spanish) : 87.4438. 000 to 448

(inset) : 87.4438.226-3

On 22nd May 2013, DBS Class 66/0 No.66013 (below) is seen in North London, crossing the Midland Main Line between Finchley Road & Frognal and West Hampstead bound fo Dollands Moor. During the summer, these trains can become more erratic on account o summer shutdowns or reduced working at Silla and Dagenham.

On 15th February 1997, Class 47/0 No.47188 (above) passes through Lenham with 7X81, the 09:33 Wembley - Dollands Moor 'Blue Train'. The loco carries 'RfD' livery; a dark grey (upper bodyside) and light grey (lower bodyside) with a logo of two red diamonds on a yellow background offset on top of a red rectangle.

On 25th January 1997, RfD Class 47/3 No.47358 (below) approaches Earls Court, viewed from Cromwel Road bridge, South Kensington, with another 7X81 service, just as a 'D' stock underground train heads towards High Street Kensington. **Nick Slocombe (5)**

Ebange Steel

The Class 92-hauled 'Ebange' steel train is a familiar sight in Kent, formed of unique 'FIA' Megafret Intermo[?]
Twin Container Flats fitted with a frame to carry steel billet. On 11th February 2012, DBS Class 92 No.920[?]
above) passes through Childsbridge with 4E32, the 11:52 Dollands Moor - Scunthorpe.   **Ian Cuthberts[?]**

This steel flow commenced in July 2003 and, excluding automotive and intermodal traffic, was the first 'blo[?]
[t]rain through the Tunnel. On 28th May 2008, Class 92 No.92009 'Elgar' (below) pilots an unidentified 92 e[?]
[o]f Paddock Wood with 6O25, the 01:39 Doncaster - Dollands Moor loaded steel.   **Alan Hazeld[?]**

Colas Steel

In March 2009, Colas Rail replaced DBS as traction provider for the weekly service of imported steel to Burton steel terminal. On 12th March 2009, Nos.47739 'Robin of Templecombe' + 47727 'Rebecca' (above) are seen crossing Eynsford Viaduct with 6Z48, 12:25 Burton - Dollands Moor steel empties. **Alan Hazelden**

On 30th April 2009, the same train is seen passing Shoreham headed by No.47739 'Robin of Templecombe' (below); a single Class 47 on this occasion due to a lighter load. As well as Nos.47727 and 47739, Colas have a third Class 47 in their fleet, No.47749 'Demelza'. This steel flow has since ceased. **Ian Cuthbertson**

Background History

National Power was formed following the privatisation of the UK electricity market in 1990.

In England and Wales, the Central Electricity Generating Board (CEGB), which was responsible for the generation and transmission of electricity, was split into four companies. Its generation activities were transferred to 'PowerGen', 'National Power', and 'Nuclear Electric' (eventually becoming 'EDF Energy'); its transmission activities going to the 'National Grid Company'.

National Power was the largest of the new companies having around 52% of the generating market. It diversified in November 1998 by purchasing the supply business of Midlands Electricity, creating 'Npower'. In October 2000, National Power demerge into 'Innogy' and 'International Power'.

April 1994

National Power enter the railfreight sector using their own fleet of Class 59/2 locos and purpose-built wagons, sporting national Power corporate blue livery. Initially, the 59/2's initial work involved carrying limestone from Tunstead to the desulphurisation plant at Drax power station, followed by 'Merry-Go-Round' coal trains from the Selby coalfield (Gascoigne Wood) to the Aire Valley power stations.

Initial Services

Limestone	: 6E56, 06:37 Tunstead - Drax	(loaded)
	6D92, 11:30 Drax ps - Ferrybridge	(empty)
	6M93, 02:18 Ferrybridge - Tunstead	(empty)

Coal : Gascoigne Wood to Drax and Eggborough power stations (Weekly Coal Plan).

59201 'Vale of York' failed at Peak Forest whilst in charge of 6E56, 06:37 Tunstead - Drax loaded limestone on the morning of 4th April 1996. Luckily, the photographer was at Edale when the train passed, having been rescued by No.59202 'Vale of White Horse', (above). It now leads, thus presenting a unique photo opportunity, as the Class 59's were seldom, if ever, operated double-headed.

59204 'Vale of Glamorgan' (opposite) leaves Drax power station on 9th July 1996 after unloading some of the 'black stuff' from Gascoigne Wood. The train is proceeding slowly along the 'Up Drax Branch', heading for the Knottingley - Goole main line.

The Aire Valley power stations consume great tonnages of coal and, by way of example, in 1997 Gascoigne Wood alone could despatch some 25 trainloads of coal a day to Drax, 5 to Eggborough and 5 to Ferrybridge. Today, in an attempt to produce 'greener' energy, Drax power station is burning biomass as an alternative to fossil fuel.   **Neil Harvey (2)**

Rolling Stock

Following Foster Yeoman, National Power investigated the possibility of running its own trains, by ordering a pilot loco - Class 59/2 No.59201. After a successful trial, five further locos were purchased, built by General Motors at their London plant in Ontario, Canada, in 1994 and 1995.

The six Class 59/2 locos differ from the other Class 59s in several ways:

- carbon dioxide fire control system, replacing the original Halon system.
- NiCd batteries instead of lead-acid.
- drop-head knuckle couplers fitted.
- advanced slow speed control for merry-go-round power station coal train operation.

A fleet of wagons were also ordered for specific flows:

Coal : 'JMA' Bogie Hopper (NP19601 - NP19682) : Built by OY Transtech in Finland.
Limestone : 'JHA' Bogie Hopper (NP19400 - NP19420) : Built by Powell Duffryn Standard.

In April 1998, EWS took over National Power rail operations and the locos were gradually repainted in EWS Maroon & Gold livery and deployed on other duties until 2005, when they were allocated to the Mendip Rail fleet.

59202 'Vale of White Horse' (above) stands in the now-demolished Gascoigne Wood complex on the 10th July 1996. The train was being loaded in readiness for its next trip to one of the nearby power stations. It's incredible to think that this once-thriving complex is now but a memory. Gascoigne Wood (near Selby) was where all the coal from pitheads at Wistow Mine, Stillingfleet Mine, Riccall Mine, North Selby Mine, Whitemoor Mine and Gascoigne Wood Mine was brought to the surface and treated before being distributed by rail. The last trainload of coal left Gascoigne Wood on 19th November 2004.

59202 'Vale of White Horse' (below) approaches Castleford Station bound for Ferrybridge p.s. on 15th May 1997. It is passing the magnificent semaphores which have now, unfortunately, been demolished. The left hand signal is an aging London and North Eastern Railway right hand bracket signal, while the signal on the right is a British Rail (Eastern Region) left hand bracket signal, installed in 1958 in conjunction with a new terminating DMU service from Leeds.

Neil Harvey (2)

'Away from Home'

59202 'Vale of White Horse' (above) was named at Didcot Power Station on 28 September 1996 by Bob Johnson, Chairman of Vale of White Horse District Council. With the huge bulk of the cooling towers dominating the background, it is pictured along with a rake of National Power 'JMA' hoppers shortly after being named. This loco was the first of the five in the production batch.

59204 'Vale of Glamorgan' (above) is seen on a dismal 16th November 1996, just as it was getting dark, passing through Barry station en-route from Yorkshire to Aberthaw Power Station, where it would be named 'Vale of Glamorgan' by the then Welsh Secretary, William Hague MP. The photographer's choice of location was deliberate, in view of the grim weather and the train's slow speed, a colour picture could be taken despite an exposure of only 1/125sec with the lens wide open!   **Martin Loader (2)**

National Power Class 59/2 Fact File

The Fleet :

No.	Works No.	Built	UK Arrival *	Ship	In Traffic
59201	918273-1	1994	16/02/1994	MV 'Haskerland'	April 1994
59202	948510-1	1995	04/08/1995	MV 'Condock V'	October 1995
59203	948510-2	1995	04/08/1995	MV 'Condock V'	16/02/1994
59204	948510-3	1995	04/08/1995	MV 'Condock V'	16/02/1994
59205	948510-4	1995	04/08/1995	MV 'Condock V'	16/02/1994
59206	948510-5	1995	04/08/1995	MV 'Condock V'	16/02/1994

* Shipped from Halifax, Nova Scotia, to Hull King George V Docks

It was originally planned for a total fleet of 12 locos but, as time proved, only six were built.

The Names :

No.	Name	Date	Named At
59201	'Vale of York'	3rd March 1994	York, National Railway Museum
59202	'Vale of White Horse'	28th September 1996	Didcot power station
59203	'Vale of Pickering'	2nd September 1995	Drax power station
59204	'Vale of Glamorgan'	18th November 1996	Aberthaw power station
59205	'Vale of Evesham' *	14th June 1996	Ferrybridge power station
59206	'Pride of Ferrybridge' **	28th June 1997	Ferrybridge depot

*   Re-named 'L. Keith McNair' on 28th March 1998 at Ferrybridge depot.

**   Originally allocated the name 'Vale of Belvoir'.

59202 **'Vale of White Horse'** (above) passes Kellingley Colliery (The "Big K") on 6th March 1997 with a Gascoigne Wood - Drax coal train. Kellingley is one of the newest of the few deep coal mines left in Britain today and started production in April 1965. It is situated next to the Aire and Calder Navigation (Knottingley & Goole Canal) and has the unique distinction of despatching coal to nearby Ferrybridge power station (about 4 miles away, as the crow flies), by barge!   **Neil Harvey**

59203 'Vale of Pickering' (above) passes Class 56 No.56093 stabled in the sidings at Sudforth Lane on the Knottingley - Goole line, as it heads back to Gascoigne Wood on 6th March 1997 to collect yet another trainload of coal for one of the Aire Valley power stations. **Neil Harvey**

59206 'Pride of Ferrybridge' (below), as yet unnamed, looks superb in its original National Power livery. It is seen passing Whitley Bridge Junction on 28 March 1997 with one of the many daily Drax power station to Gascoigne Wood coal empties, using National Power's own dedicated hoppers. The loco is named 'Pride of Ferrybridge' at the eponymous depot exactly three months later. **Martin Loader**

59205 'Vale of Evesham' (above) passes a popular spot for enthusiasts, Milford Junction. On 10th July 1996, No.59205 heads along the 'Up Pontefract' line with a trainload of the 'black stuff' destined for Drax power station, which will be routed via Ferrybridge North Junction, Knottingley, Hensall and Drax Branch Junction.

59201 'Vale of York' (below) passes Hensall Station (note the steps for passengers on the low platforms) on 19th March 1998 heading for Drax with loaded coal. When the 'Vale' theme was adopted for naming, it was appropriate that the first loco should be named 'Vale of York, considering the loco's planned area of use and National Power's base in Yorkshire.   **Neil Harvey (2)**

A Veritable Feast of Traction

Background

With a continuing upsurge in freight traffic, greater demands are being placed on motive power, so much so that train operators are having to rely on their own fleet of 'heritage' traction to satisfy demand; even to the extent of hiring traction from private concerns.

Infrastructure, departmental and engineer's trains are a prime candidate for such traction.

Motive Power

The locos made available vary considerably: 20s, 31s, 33s, 37s, 47s, 56s readily spring to mind and GBRf have even trialled a Class 52 'Western'!

Engineer's 'trips' and scheduled WTT departmental services attract considerable interest among rail enthusiasts and this portfolio illustrates the variety. However, as GBRf Class 73s are a common sight on such workings around the old Southern Region, this loco class has been excluded from this portfolio.

As most of these services work out of designated Local Distribution Centres (LDC) and Virtual Quarries (VQ), a map has been included (left) to show their locations.

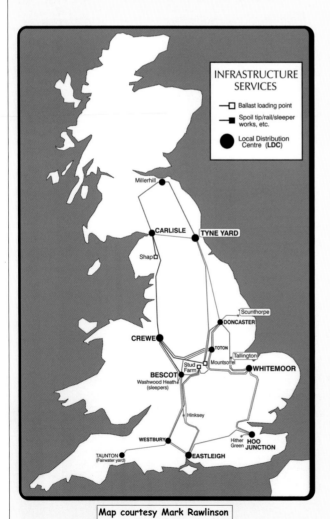

Map courtesy Mark Rawlinson

(Opposite)
North East 'Choppers'
6T27
Doncaster Decoy - Heighington

20312 + 20303 (top right) stand at Heighington station on the Darlington - Bishop Auckland branch with 6T27, Doncaster Decoy Yard - Heighington steel sleeper laying train, awaiting permission to enter the engineer's possession.

20303 (middle) is seen again, standing at Newton Aycliffe station, just south of the engineering possession, with a solitary wagon from the sleeper laying train.

20303 (bottom) is shut down and tails No.20312, standing in the 'Up/Down' passing loop at Darlington station.

The train is en route to Heighington and consists of the Balfour Beatty RS Harsco Track Technologies New Track Construction Machine, for relaying new sleepers and rail on to a pre-prepared track bed.   **Ian Ball (3)**

20302 + 37611 (above) drop down Shap passing Scout Green on a dull 17th December 2013 with 6C27, the 09:42 Carlisle Yard - Shap Quarry, via Tebay, empty ballast tipplers. This rare 20 + 37 combination was instead of the normal 'booked' DRS Class 66/4 traction. **Keith McGovern**

33029 (below) hired in from WCRC, passes through North Camp station on 9th January with an engineer's train, running as 6Z47, Westbury - Woking. The former Eastleigh-based 'crompton', named 'Glen Loy', is hauling a 'ZOA-K' Kirow KRC250UK Heavy Duty Diesel Hydraulic Crane. **Simon Howard**

On Track Plant & Departmental 'Trips'

The 'Railvac'

Numbers : 99.70.9515.001-4
99.70.9515.002-2

Description

The 'RA7' RAILVAC™ is Railcare AB's first bespoke air/vacuum excavator; its full name:

Ballast Vacuum Extraction System (BVES)

Designed and built in partnership with the DISAB Group of Sweden, it conforms with the UK's W6A loading gauge standards. The 'RA7' can be towed DIT in a train formation and, when in a track possession, it can work in self-propelled mode, classified as On Track Plant (OTP).

A Network Rail Engineering Acceptance Certificate (EAC) was issued in 2012 and the unit can now provide ballast excavation services all over the rail network.

Operation

The RA7's suction comes from two Caterpillar C9 diesel engines, two vacuum pumps and two air compressors, creating 19,000 cubic metres of air flow per hour. The machine has a manipulator arm for excavation and a unique hydrostatic transmission system that is powerful, reliable and precise in its operation. 'RA7' excavation applications include:

- Cribbing and undercutting mainline mud spots.
- Removing fouled ballast and debris.
- Cleaning and installing drain tiles and culverts.
- Cross trenching for cables and pipes.
- Undercutting switches and diamonds.
- Excavating contaminated materials from yards and stations.

(**Above**) : RAILVAC No.99.70.9515.001-4   Eastleigh   **Simon Howard**

'RAILVAC' 20142 + 20189 (above) provide a rare freight move over the Chiltern line on 31st March when Nos.20142 and 20189 (on hire to DCR) work 6Z20, 12:00 Derby Chaddesden Sidings - Willesden Euroterminal 'Railvac' move. Running a couple of minutes late, the train heads south on the 'Up' main line through Princes Risborough station. **Geoff Plumb**

56312, after a weekend over the festive period 'hoovering' up ballast in Fife, the Swedish Railvac has to return south. It is seen here being hauled by DCR Class 56 No.56312 (below) in near darkness at 09:15hrs on the morning of 2nd January. The train is crossing the River Esk viaduct, just under seven miles north of Carlisle, known locally as the Metal Bridge. The train is running as 6Z42, Mossend - Totton Yard. **Guy Houston**

1190 (above) sits in the middle road at Carlisle Citadel station on 13th January, having arrived on the Sunday afternoon (12th) with 6Z42, Millerhill - Taunton . However, as the driver did not know the alternative route via he 'S & C', there was no choice but to hold the train at Carlisle until the WCML re-opened. The WCML had losed north of Penrith the previous day due to a collision involving two engineer's trains (6L42 and 6L43). he Swedish railvac is number 99.70.9515.001-4. **Guy Houston**

0142 + 20189 (below) are out again on 30th March and this time they are seen passing Duffield on the Derby Sheffield main line with a special 6Z20, Maltby Colliery - Chaddesden sidings. The leading loco displays a eadcode of 1K73, which is clearly incorrect! **Jamie Squibbs**

56303 (above) is an impressive sight, passing Scout Green on the 1 in 75 descent towards Tebay with 6Z34, the 09:15 Shap Quarry - Foxton loaded stone. This 'STP' working utilises a rake of internationally registered 'JRA' Bogie Box Wagons in the 70.6790.000 - 70.6790.099 series. **Keith McGovern**

56094 (below) sits at Platform 2 of Glasgow Central station on 15th December 2013 at one end of 6Y82, Eglinton Street - Mossend engineer's train, having worked overnight in a possession on the East Kilbride branch. It needed to reverse in Glasgow Central with a hired in DBS Class 66/0 No.66025, on the other end, to drag the train away from the station. **Guy Houston**

56103

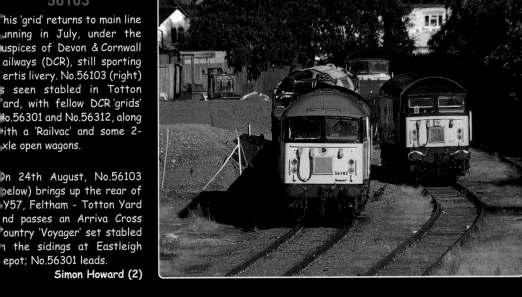

This 'grid' returns to main line running in July, under the auspices of Devon & Cornwall Railways (DCR), still sporting Fertis livery. No.56103 (right) is seen stabled in Totton Yard, with fellow DCR 'grids' No.56301 and No.56312, along with a 'Railvac' and some 2-axle open wagons.

On 24th August, No.56103 (below) brings up the rear of 6Y57, Feltham - Totton Yard and passes an Arriva Cross Country 'Voyager' set stabled in the sidings at Eastleigh Depot; No.56301 leads.

Simon Howard (2)

The Fertis livery is similar to Railfreight Grey, comprising light grey (almost white!) with dark grey roof and red solebar. No.56078 was actually the first loco to receive the Fertis livery in June 2004.

For the record : This livery was applied to those locos sent to France to work on the construction of the new LGV est high speed line between Paris and Strasbourg, which opened in 2007.

Following the successful hire of Class 37s to Spain, France and Italy, plus 58s to Spain and the Netherlands, EWS was keen to secure more work overseas for their stored, but perfectly serviceable, locos following the introduction of the Class 66s. For the LGV est line, SNCF appointed Fertis, the French rail infrastructure company, to supply the traction for ballast trains. Fertis hired 40 locomotives from EWS, in the shape of 26 Class 56s and 14 Class 58s.

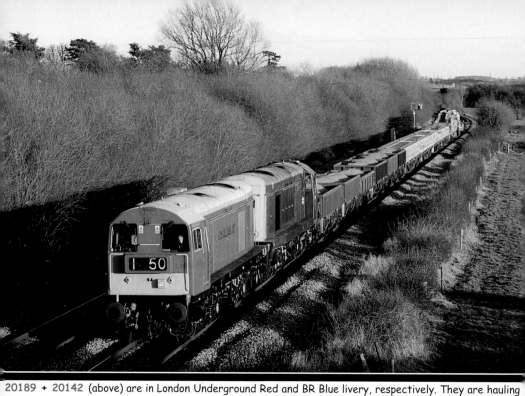

20189 + 20142 (above) are in London Underground Red and BR Blue livery, respectively. They are hauling 6K50, the 15:13 Toton - Crewe Basford Hall on 7th February, seen in superb, almost autumn-like, early evening light at Barrow upon Trent. This turn would normally be a GBRf Class 66/7 loco.   **Jamie Squibbs**

57003 + 57007 (below) cross Ribblehead Viaduct on 12th March, substituting for the usual 'Dred' (Class 66/4) with 6K05, the 12:46 Carlisle Yard - Crewe Basford Hall, on a day when the photographer could not remember seeing the light quite so crystal clear in this part of the world.   **Neil Harvey**

37405 + 37423 'Spirit Of The Lakes' + 37610 'T.S.(Ted) Cassidy' (above) climb Wilpshire Bank with another 6K05 departmental service from Carlisle to Crewe on 28th February; photographers hoping for 'tractors' on this train at some point, but no-one expects three to turn up at once! **Neil Harvey**

Transformation .... Nos. 20189 + 20142 are now adorned in Balfour Beatty livery. On 9th May, as an 'Up' East Coast express rapidly approaches, Nos.20189 + 20142 (below) pass New Zealand Bridge on the approach to Sandy with 6Z20, 13:00 Stapleford & Sandacre - Langley (Bucks). **Nigel Gibbs**

37405 + **37608** (above) pile on the power as they power through Kingsbury on a murky 5th May with 6Z96, the 12:22 Crewe VQ - Toton departmental; a service acquired by DRS from DBS and booked a DRS Class 66/4 loco. This is the junction where Kingsbury oil trains and scrap metal services access their respective terminals, plus Birch Coppice intermodal traffic.   **Craig Adamson**

47843 'Vulcan' + **57312 'Peter Henderson'** (below) are hired by GBRf from Riviera Trains and Network Rail, respectively, to work 6K50, the 15:13 Toton - Crewe Basford Hall on 28th March. The colourful combination are seen at Stenson Bubble, awaiting a path south.   **Jamie Squibbs**

Anglo-Scottish Departmental
Electric Traction

Background

The only departmental service 'booked' for electric traction is an out & back 'trip' between Carlisle Yard and Mossend Yard, operated by GBRf using a Class 92 loco. The service is:

6M49, 08:21 Mossend - Carlisle Yard   **6S51, 12:16 Carlisle Yard - Mossend**

When you consider that all other such services, including weekend engineer's trains, are usually diesel hauled, these two workings are certainly a rarity:

31st December 2013   -   **6M49 / 6S51** :   86605 + 86632

2nd January 2014   -   **6M49 / 6S51** :   87002 + 92010

Selective Images : (Overleaf) **Guy Houston (2)**

31st December 2013 : With resident GBRf Class 92 No.92010 'Moliere' declared a failure with various faults, Freightliner are asked to provide alternative traction, and this is the result. A rare sight of a pair of Class 86/6s on a ballast train! Nos.86605 + 86632 (Page 69) cross Crawford Viaduct in the Upper Clyde Valley with 6S51, the 12:16 Carlisle Yard - Mossend. The payload of 15 wagons weighs in at just 282 tonnes (442 tonnes including the locos) and the consist is:

FDA: 621486 / 621530	YMA: 996360	MHA : 394087 / 394866
MHA : 394234 / 394095 / 394019 / 394155 / 394644 / 394943 / 394355 / 394963 / 394021 / 394726		

As a pair of Class 86s are restricted to a trailing load of 1,260 tonnes on this stretch of line, an additional train (6Z57 with 1,347 tonnes, including locos) is put on to move the balance of the consist. Train 6Z57 is worked by a pair of DRS Class 57 locos No.57011 + No,57009, consisting of 2 x 5 vehicle sets of 'HQA' and 1 x 5 vehicle 'JJA' set of autoballasters.

2nd January 2014 : If a pair of Freightliner 86s isn't rare enough, GBRf go one better with a pairing of Class 87 No.87002 'Royal Sovereign' + Class 92 No.92010 'Moliere'. The class 92 has a faulty wiper which needs replacing but, due to the holiday period, there are no spares close by and a replacement loco needs to be sourced. Here, Nos.87002 + 92010 (Page 68), both providing power, head 6M49, the 08:22 Mossend - Carlisle Yard on the last leg of the journey crossing the River Esk at Metal Bridge, Carlisle. The consist of 1,598 tonnes is:

IEA : 70.5892.010-7	KFA : 97408 / 97414	MLA : 503122 / 503114
YSA : 996849	YWA : 996627	ZOA : 81621 / 81623
JNA : 29478 / 29005 / 29064 / 29176 / 29499 / 29254 / 29514 / 29431 / 29456 / 29255		

(Above) : Class 87 No.87002 + Class 92 No.92010 are seen approaching Carstairs on 2nd January with 6S51, the 12:16 Carlisle Yard - Mossend Yard departmental service.   **Alastair Blackwood**

(Above) : No.87002 + No.92010 Metal Bridge, Carlisle

(Below) : Nos.86605 + 86632 Crawford Viaduct, Upper Clyde Valley

"Just Champion"….

D1015 'Western Champion' (above), clearly running on two engines, waits to follow a London St Pancras - Sheffield passenger service onto the 'Down Fast' line at Harrowden Junction (26th November 2013) with a rake of VTG 'JNA' Bogie Open Box Wagons, which form 6D02, the 11:21 Wellingborough - Mountsorrrel.

Now on its way, a very back-lit glint shot of 'Wizzo' No.D1015 'Western Champion' (below) crossing onto the 'Down Fast' at Harrowden Junction with full clag - 'Maybach Music' indeed.

Meanwhile, still on hire to GBRf, No.D1015 (above) propels its train out of Finedon Road Yard, Wellingborough, on 5th December 2013; 6D02, the 11.21 ballast empties to Mountsorrel which, on this occasion, is formed of the 'PHA' Self-Discharge Train. The consist is made up of 'PHA-P' (Basic Hopper), 'PHA-Q' (Basic Hopper with Generator), 'PHA-R' (Basic Hopper fitted with Belt Tensioner), 'PHA-S' (Basic Hopper Generator) wagons and a 'KJA' Discharge Wagon in the middle of the train set.

Beforehand, the BR 'Western class' diesel hydraulic loco (below) poses in the low winter sun at Finedon Road, prior to coupling up to its train. **Nigel Gibbs (4)**

Background

In May, DRS unveil a variation of their 'Flying Compass' branding on Class 37/4 No.37423 'Spirit of the Lakes' (see opposite), similar to that applied to the new DRS Class 68 locos; the first Class 37 to receive this livery.

First Run

On 22nd April, No.37423 returns to mainline action after overhaul at Eastleigh, albeit without DRS branding and nameplate, taking a new DRS Class 68 (No.68002) to Crewe. The following weekend, No.37423 (still unbranded) assists sister Class 37/0 No.37259 on railtour duties between Crewe and the Kyle of Lochalsh.

Interim DRS livery : On 22nd April, unbranded and minus nameplates, No.37423 (above) passes through Kensington Olympia towing Vossloh 'UKlight' Class 68 loco, No.68002 'Intrepid'. The train is 0Z68, the 11:32 Eastleigh Works - Willesden Brent. **Nigel Gibbs**

Profile History

Built	English Electric Vulcan Works, Newton-Le-Willows		
In Traffic	July 1965		
Number	D6996 (From New)	37296 (January 1974)	37423 (January 1986)

Livery

From New	BR Brunswick Green	September 1989	InterCity Mainline
January 1974	BR Blue	October 1994	Two-Tone Grey / Transrail branding
July 1985	BR Blue, Large Logo	December 2007	DRS Blue, Compass Livery
February 1988	Experimental Two-Tone Grey	April 2014	Revised DRS Compass Livery
May 1988	Railfreight Two-Tone Grey		

Allocations

July 1965	Cardiff Canton	May 1997	Crewe Diesel Depot
October 1977	Landore, Swansea	July 1997	Stratford
October 1980	Bristol Bath Road	September 1997	Toton
November 1981	Landore	November 1998	Motherwell
January 1984	Cardiff Canton	November 1999	Headquarters (Stored)
January 1985	Eastfield, Glasgow	December 2007	Carlisle Kingmoor
August 1992	Motherwell		

Names

May 1988	'Sir Murray Morrison - 1873-1948 Pioneer of British Aluminium Industry'
July 2009	'Spirit of the Lakes'

BR Blue : Prior to succumbing to the ETH-fitted programme in January 1996, this loco became No.37296 under TOPS in January 1974. Here, No.37296 (above) enters Tyndrum Upper station on the West Highland Line on 5th February 1985 with 7D12, the 12:19 Fort William - Mossend 'Speedlink', the first three wagons are 2-axle 'OBAs', used to bring pulp to the paper mill at Corpach.   **John Baker**

Forty Years On : DRS 'Flying Compass' livery : No.37423 'Spirit of the Lakes' (above), sporting the new corporate colours, passes Dawlish on 15th May hauling a Ministry of Defence sponsored 6Z40, the 09:39 Crewe Coal Sidings - Devonport Royal Dockyard; fuel for nuclear submarines.

Following storm damage in February, the line re-opens on 4th April and, excluding engineer's trains, the first trains to pass Dawlish were two ECS services; a nine car Voyager forming 5Z66, 23:45 Exeter St. Davids - Laira and a Class 150/1 unit, running as 5Z46, 00.02 Newton Abbot - Exeter. **Robert Sherwood**

Livery Perspectives

InterCity Mainline : Between September 1989 and October 1994, No.37423 carried this particular livery, as we can see on No.37423 'Sir Murray Morrison' (above) waiting to leave Oban on 26th August 1992 with 7D23, the 09:30 empty fuel oil tanks to Mossend. The notable landmark of McCaig's folly stands proudly on the hill above the town.   **Chris Perkins**

BR Blue, Large Logo : On 31st October 1987, No.37423 (below) is stabled at Eastfield TMD, Glasgow, awaiting its next turn of duty. Of note, Eastfield was one of the first depots to adopt a mascot logo, the West Highland terrier or 'Scottie Dog', which it applied to the bodyside of its locos.   **Martin Buck**

Two-Tone Grey : Simply stunning! Sporting two-tone grey livery with BR trainload freight decals of Yellow & Blue chevrons, representing the metals sector, No.37423 'Sir Murray Morrison' (above) hauls its train across Rannoch Viaduct on 21st July 1988; 1D15, the 17:45 Fort William - Mossend, a 'portion' which will be added to 1M16 ex-Inverness for the overnight run to London Euston.

Transrail : No.37423 was in Transrail livery for over 12 years and it could be found working passenger services to Holyhead, Rhymney and Weymouth. On 25th July 1999, No.37423 'Sir Murray Morrison' (below) climbs towards Pilning with 2O87, the 07:45 (SU) Cardiff Central - Weymouth. **John Chalcraft (2)**

The Return

In April, Class 50 No.50007 returns to action sporting BR Blue livery and 'Hercules' nameplates after being sold by the Class Forty Appeal to Boden Rail Engineering Ltd in September 2013. Perhaps, it is just a coincidence but No.50007 makes a comeback as 'Hercules' in the same year that a blockbuster film is scheduled for release, directed by Brett Ratner; *"Hercules"*, based on the graphic novel *"Hercules: The Thracian Wars"*.

On 2nd April, No.50007 travels to the Mid-Norfolk Railway, in a convoy led by Class 52 No.D1015 'Western Champion', Class 37 No.37219 and Class 40 No.D306 'Atlantic Conveyor'.

This loco was probably the most talked about and divisive member of the 50-strong fleet due to it being repainted in GWR Brunswick Green Livery and fitted with brass nameplate, number, crest and arrows in 1984. The 'Hoover' purists certainly didn't take to it!

First Run on the Main Line

17th May : 6E07, the 08:59 Washwood Heath - Boston Docks

Profile History

Built	: English Electric Vulcan Works, Newton-Le-Willows	
In Traffic	: March 1968	
Number	: From New	: D407
	April 1974	: 50007
Livery	: From New	: BR Blue
	March 1983	: BR Blue, Large Logo
	February 1984	: GWR Brunswick Green
	April 2014	: BR Blue
Allocations	: March 1968	: London Midland Region (Western Lines)
	June 1968	: D05 Stoke-on-Trent Division
	May 1973	: Crewe TMD
	May 1974	: Plymouth Laira TMD
Names	: April 1978	: 'Hercules'
	February 1984	: 'Sir Edward Elgar'
Withdrawn	: March 1994	
Preserved	: July 1994	The Class 40 Appeal - Midland Railway Centre

Notes

(1) The loco was named after HMS Hercules, a Colossus-class battleship built by Palmers, launched on 10th May 1910 and commissioned on 31 July 1911 at Portsmouth. She was a 20,000-ton 'dreadnought', mounting ten 12 inch guns.

(2) It is the only Class 50 to haul the Royal Train.
5th May 1987, taking HRH Prince Charles from London Paddington to Totnes.

(3) 26th March 1994 : Final Class 50 working - '50 Terminator' railtour.
No.50007 + No.50050 working London Waterloo - Penzance - London Paddington.

Craig Adamson

50007

1984 - 2014

Thirty years ago, Class 50 No.50007 'Hercules' was repainted GWR Brunswick Green and named 'Sir Edward Elgar'; three decades later, it reappears in original BR Blue livery and carrying 'Hercules' nameplates.

On 17th May, No.50007 (above) passes Barton Central Rivers on its maiden run back on the main line. Coupled immediately behind No.50007 is Colas Class 56 No.56105, which is to be given a test run on the return working. At the rear of the train, which consists of ten empty 'IHA' covered steel carriers, is Class 47/7 No.47739 'Robin of Templecombe 1938-2013', provided for insurance. **John Whitehouse**

Later into the outward journey, No.50007 'Hercules' (below) thunders through the Leicestershire countryside near Muston (between Bottesford and Grantham) with 6E07 to Boston Docks. **James Welham**

'The Green Era' : A far cry from its glory days as a passenger loco, No.50007 'Sir Edward Elgar' (above) ambles down the relief line at Pilning on 13th March 1989 with a train of track panels destined for South Wales. No.50007 was only allocated to the DCWA engineer's pool for a short while (8th October 1988 to 14th May 1989), so pictures of it on such mundane duties while in BR service are not common. **Martin Loader**

On 7th July 1984, green liveried and spotlight-fitted, No.50007 'Sir Edward Elgar' (below) passes Cowley Bridge Junction with the 17:45hrs Paignton - London Paddington. Semaphore signalling was replaced by MAS (Multiple Aspect Signalling) on 1st April 1985 when Exeter signalling centre opened. **John Chalcraft**

A meeting of two 'classic' loco classes at Hungerford Common on 3rd September 1984. Brunswick Green No.50007 'Sir Edward Elgar' (above) heads west with the 09:40hrs London Paddington - Penzance, while Class47/0 No.47240 passes with the 06:28hrs Penzance - Paddington, vice HST.

50007 'Sir Edward Elgar' (below), now preserved, approaches Quorn & Woodhouse with 2A30, the 14:25 Loughborough - Leicester North, during the Great Central Railway's Diesel Gala on 12th September 2009. This loco was the highlight of the event, the GCR had never hosted a Class 50 before.   **Martin Loader (2)**

'The Blue Era' : A shabby looking No.50007 'Hercules' (above) passes Berkley, near Frome, on 29th August 1981 with the St. Austell - London Paddington Motorail service. Motorail ceased in 1995 when British Rail was privatised. First Great Western relaunched a service from London Paddington to Penzance as part of their Night Riviera overnight sleeper service in 1999, but withdrew it at the end of summer 2005.

No.50007 'Hercules' (below) exits the west portal of the 264 yards long Twerton Tunnel on 12th May 1980 with 1B72, the 12:20 London Paddington - Bristol Temple Meads. The tunnel was built 1836 - 1840 by Isambard Kingdom Brunel, and the portals at either end are of Tudor Gothic style and are listed.   **John Chalcraft (2)**

50007 'Hercules' (above) breasts the summit at Whiteball on 9th April 1982 with the 10:28hrs London Paddington - Exeter St. Davids, having just exited the west portal of Whiteball Tunnel. The driver can now ease off the power, as it's downhill all the way to Exeter.   **John Chalcraft**

A busy time at Oxford on 2nd April 1983. In BR Blue Large Logo livery, No.50007 'Hercules' (below) departs with 1V68, the 08:20 Liverpool Lime Street - London Paddington, which it had worked from Birmingham New Street. Class 47 No.47559 arrives at Platform 2 with 1M50, the 09:00 Brighton - Manchester Piccadilly. A Class 121 'bubble car' waits in the down carriage siding with its trailer No.54281 (L281).   **Martin Loader**

State of Play

Class 56s 06:00hrs, Thursday, 2nd January 2014

Number	Pool	Location	Status	Allocated
COLAS				
56049	COLO	Washwood Heath	B - Not to be moved	
56051	COLO	Washwood Heath	D - At TMD awaiting maintenance	
56078	COLO	Washwood Heath	N - Normal (available for traffic)	6M08 (arr.)
56087	COLO	Washwood Heath	N - Normal (available for traffic)	
56090	COLO	Washwood Heath	B - Not to be moved	
56094	COLO	Burton on Trent	N - Normal (available for traffic)	6Z47
56096	COLO	Washwood Heath	B - Not to be moved	
56105	COLO	Bo'ness	N - Normal (available for traffic)	6R46
56113	COLO	Eastleigh	N - Normal (available for traffic)	6Z29
56302	COLO	Burton WS	N - Normal (available for traffic)	6Z47

Allocations : 6M08, Boston Docks - Washwood Heath   6Z47, Burton WS - Taunton Fairwater Yard
             6R46, Grangemouth - Prestwick   6Z29, Newton Abbot - Westbury Yard

Portfolio

A selection of contrasting images, with the spotlight falling on Nos.56078, 56096 and 56113.

6V62 : A pair of 'grids' on the GWML. Nos.56113 + 56094 (above) pass Grove foot Crossing on the 'Down Main', 15th February, with 6V62, 11:12 Tilbury - Llanwern empty steel carriers. At this point the ex-GWR main line runs as four track for four miles between Wantage Road and Challow.   **Simon Howard**

6N72 : Meanwhile, the weather looks disappointingly gloomy in Scotland on Wednesday, 19th March, when No.56078 (top right) passes through Leuchars with 6N72, the 14:48 Linkswood - Grangemouth empty fuel oil tanks. The 'grids', along with Colas Class 47/7s and Class 66/8s, have regular duties out of Grangemouth to Linkswood (6R46), Prestwick (6R46) and Sinfin (6M65).   **Jim Ramsay**

6Z31 : Ah, some sunshine! An immaculate No.56078 (bottom right) leads No.56113 out of Eastleigh Yard on 11th January with an early running 6Z31, the 20:31hrs departmental to Westbury. There is plenty of loco activity in the yard; two DBS Class 66/0s, a Class 60 and a Class 08 shunter.   **Simon Howard**

6M54 : The brightly coloured oilseed rape is starting to lose its brilliance but is, nevertheless, still a sight to behold. No.56113 (above) sweeps past the colourful vista at Llanellen, Abergavenny, on 15th April with 6M54, the 15:26 Baglan Bay - Chirk loaded timber.   **Jamie Squibbs**

6O26 : Colas Class 56 No.56113 (above) passes through Swindon on 27th December 2013 with 6O26, the 10:19 departmental service from Hinksey, running to Westbury instead of Eastleigh on this occasion. The 'grid' has been hired by Freightliner to cover a loco shortage.

This image brings back memories for the author. He worked during the '70s' and early '80s for a leading insurance company, who had an office on the top floor of the building on the right, affording great views of the approaches to Swindon station. A lunchtime would often result in a stroll to this same spot to photograph a Class 50 on 1B72 to Bristol Temple Meads or a pair of Class 37s working 6B08 empty petroleum tanks from Langley back to Robeston. Those were the days!   **Steven King**

6V37 : No.56078 in trouble .... On 28th April, exhaust plumes drift away from No.56087 (above) as it heads off into the distance towards Blea Moor to run round 6V37, the 14:42 Ribblehead VQ - Chirk logs, which is running some 78 minutes late. Colas Class 47/7 No.47739 'Robin Of Templecombe' + Class 56 No.56078 (DIT) are on the rear of the train which is crossing Ribblehead Viaduct. No.56078 had failed and Nos.47739 and 56087 were sent light engine (0Z56) from Washwood Heath to effect a rescue. **Neil Harvey**

4Z63 : Colas Rail are available for 'spot hire' work, like on 22nd April, when No.56113 (below) is seen passing Bishton signal box taking a single coal hopper to Stoke Gifford; the train is 4Z63, 13:30hrs ex-Cardiff Canton. The signal box now only controls the level crossing, although there is a nearby underbridge for road traffic, which only has a headroom of 5ft 6ins. At night the signal box is not open. **Jamie Squibbs**

56078 + 56113 (above) are allocated to work 6M54, the 14:55 Baglan Bay - Chirk loaded timber on 13th May, which is seen at Cheney Longville, near Craven Arms. Note the ex-GWR lower quadrant semaphore signals mounted on separate posts (dolls) on a bracket. The right-hand arm applies to the main line and the left-hand arm serves the 'Down Goods Loop'. The arms are at differing heights, the highest one indicates the faster route.   **Mike Hemming**

(Previously) : 'April Fools Day' .... No.56078 (Page 86) passes Northgate Locks, Chester, running one hour early with 6J37, Preston Skew Bridge - Chirk loaded timber. The train is actually 24-hours late as No.56078 was declared a failure en-route from Carlisle at Preston the previous day, where it recessed at Skew Bridge pending the attention of the fitter. The train is heading for Saltney Junction where it will leave the North Wales main line for Chirk, via the single line to Wrexham General.   **Colin Partington**

A delightful scene; No.56113 (Page 87) ambles along the branch at Heathfield, near Newton Abbot on 23rd July with 6V54, the 06:10 Chirk Kronospan - Teigngrace empty timber carriers. The loading point at Teigngrace is 2 miles and 28 chains from Heathfield Branch Junction.   **Peter Slater**

56096

6V38 : The latest Colas 'grid' to return to traffic in 2014 is a former 'Fertis' machine, No.56096. On 13th September, an immaculate No.56096 (above) is seen double-headed with No.56105 roaring through Long Preston with 6V38, the 14:52 Ribblehead VQ - Chirk loaded timber. **Neil Harvey**

6V62 : On 12th August, the driver piles on the power as No.56096 (below) accelerates through Water Orton with 6E07, the 14:50 Washwood Heath - Boston Docks steel empties. It's running on the main line via Lea Marston, as opposed to the slower route (on the left) via Whitacre Junction. **Steven Brykajlo**

6Z43

Just about one hour after leaving Llanwern Exchange Sidings, No.56113 (left) gingerly makes its way along the 'freight only' branch on 1st March, from Alexandra Dock Junction towards the dock entrance with a trainload of steel, running as 6Z43, the 11:30 Llanwern Exchange Sidings - Newport Docks.

Having arrived back at Llanwern with the 6Z42 empties from Newport Docks, it's time to work another 'trip'. No.56113 (opposite) crawls towards the signal which controls access to the South Wales Main Line with 6Z43, 11:30 Llanwern - Newport Docks..

In the event, the third round trip of the day didn't run.

6Z42

Super composition .... on 1st March, No.56113 (above) passes the site of East Usk signal box, Newport, with 6Z42, the 09:46 Newport Docks - Llanwern steel empties. At the same time, an unidentified Class 66/0 makes its way into the yard to reverse with yet more export steel from Llanwern to Birdport, a steel terminal on the east bank of the River Usk.   **Nick Slocombe (3)**

Llanwern - Newport Docks
Steel Exports

The Work
Colas Rail are often called upon to work STP 'trips' in South Wales moving trainloads of steel from Llanwern steelworks to Newport Docks for export, work suitable for one of their Class 56s, as is the case during February and March.

The 'Trips'
The loaded 'trip' takes about 60 minutes to complete and here is the diagram:

0Z41, 05:45   **Canton Sidings - Llanwern Exchange Sidings**
6Z41, 07:09   Llanwern Exchange Sidings - Newport Docks
6Z42, 09:46   **Newport Docks - Llanwern Exchange Sidings**
6Z43, 11:30   Llanwern Exchange Sidings - Newport Docks
6Z44, 14:15   **Newport Docks - Llanwern Exchange Sidings**
6Z45, 15:55   Llanwern Exchange Sidings - Newport Docks
6Z46, 19:15   **Newport Docks - Llanwern Exchange Sidings**
0Z46, 20:38   **Llanwern Exchange Sidings - Cardiff Canton**

6Z43
Timings

LLANWERN EXCHANGE SIDINGS	**11:30**
Llanwern West Junction	11:47
Maindee West Junction	11:53
NEWPORT	11:58
Alexandra Dock Junction	12:01
NEWPORT DOCKS	**12:29**

"All Present and Correct"

DBS start 2014 with a fleet of **26** Class 60s - **ALL** actually in traffic - the highest number since DBS instigated the 'Super 60' overhaul schedule.

Here is the state of play, **Thursday, 2nd January 2014** :

Number	Pool	Location	Allocation
60001	WCAT	Immingham	6M99, Rotherham - Wolverhampton
60007	WCBT	Peak Forest	
60010	WCBT	Warrington Arpley	6F78, Fiddlers Ferry - Liverpool BKTM
60011	WCBT	Doncaster	
60015	WCBT	Peak Forest	
60017	WCBT	Toton	
60019	WCAT	Doncaster	
60020	WCBT	Warrington Arpley	
60024	WCAT	Liverpool BKTM	6F74, Liverpool BKTM - Fiddlers Ferry
60039	WCAT	Margam	
60040	WCAT	Theale	6B33, Theale - Robeston
60044	WCAT	Immingham	6M24, Lindsey - Kingsbury
60045	WCAT	Eastleigh	
60054	WCBT	Rectory Junction	6E82, Rectory Junction - Lindsey
60059	WCBT	Kingsbury	6E59, Kingsbury - Lindsey
60062	WCAT	Margam	6E30, Margam - Hartlepool
60063	WCAT	Immingham	
60065	WCAT	Doncaster	
60066	WCAT	Margam	6A11, Robeston - Theale
60071	WCBT	Lackenby	6D11, Lackenby - Scunthorpe
60074	WCAT	Immingham Ore Terminal	6T25, Immingham - Scunthorpe Santon
60079	WCAT	Washwood Heath	
60091	WCBT	Lindsey	6V70, Lindsey - Colnbrook
60092	WCBT	Toton	
60099	WCAT	Westerleigh	6B47, Westerleigh - Robeston
60100	WCAT	Kingsbury	6E54, Kingsbury - Humber

Pool Codes :

WCAT : Class 60 Normal Fuel Capacity   **WCBT** : Class 60 Extra Fuel Capacity

Portfolio

It seems hard to believe that at the start of 2010, only *five* Class 60s were in traffic: 60009 / 60049 / 60059 / 60071 and 60096; photographers busy seeking out that elusive 'tug' shot.

Now, the DBS Class 60 fleet is stable and 60s have become a regular sight across the rail network, especially with so many 'pink' examples (DBS red 60s, christened 'pink' by enthusiasts) in service. Their rarity value has diminished and so, in this particular issue of *LR*, we seek out some 'alternative' locations, plus profiling Nos.**60044** and **60066**.

(Opposite)

(Top Right) : The **EWS 'Beasties'** decal was added later. No.60044 is seen in its final guise prior to 'Super Tug' conversion, passing East Usk, Newport, on 8th August 2006 with 6M41, the 12:22 Margam - Round Oak loaded steel. Eight years later, the Mainline Aircraft Blue livery is no more, as is the ex-GWR semaphore signal controlling the line to Birdport steel terminal.   **Martin Buck**

(Middle) : Following overhaul, No.60044 is seen at Toton TMD on 15th December 2013.   **Craig Adamson**

(Bottom Right) : No.60044 approaches the A18 road bridge at Melton Ross, where the lime works form an impressive backdrop. The 'pink' tug is working 6T24, the 11:41 Immingham - Santon on 24th March and the black stuff in the third wagon doesn't much look like iron ore!   **Neil Harvey**

'Tug' Profile

60044

In Traffic
July 1991

Depot Allocation
July 1991	:	Toton
September 1991	:	Thornaby
July 1992	:	Toton
November 2000	:	Thornaby
May 2004	:	Immingham

Livery
July 1991	:	Two-Tone Grey
February 1996	:	Mainline Blue
December 2013	:	DBS Red

Names
November 1990	:	'Ailsa Craig'

Withdrawn
June 2006

Reinstated
December 2013

60044

BR Trainload Metals
Two Tone Grey
Yellow & Blue Chevrons logo

No.60044 'Ailsa Craig' (top left) at Immingham TMD. **Ian Cuthbertson**

BR Mainline Freight
Two Tone Grey
"rolling wheels" logo

A clean looking 60044 'Ailsa Craig' (middle) approaches Wolvercote Junction on 30 June 1995 with 6M58, the 17:25 Didcot Power Station - Toton MGR empties.

The interim Mainline Freight livery was the blandest of the privatised freight company's colour schemes, made even more so by the omission of the 'Mainline' wording, which was normally applied below the logo.

EWS 'Beasties'

On 2nd April 2007, No.60044 (below) leans into the curve at Kintbury on the 'Berks & Hants' line with 6Z20, 09:45 Whatley - St. Pancras loaded stone hoppers. This is a very odd combination of liveries, with an EWS branded Mainline Blue loco hauling a rake of ex-National Power hoppers!

Martin Loader (2)

BR Mainline Freight :
'Aircraft Blue'
silver bodyside stripe, "rolling wheels" logo

Circa June 2004 : No.60044 (above), devoid of nameplates, passes over the River Dun Navigation Canal at Kirk Sandall with 6D65, the 10:07 Doncaster - Immingham 'Enterprise'.

The consist includes 'BEA'-style Bogie Bolsters and 'BYA' Telescopic Coil Carriers, plus some 2-Axle 'VGA' vans at the rear of the train; the latter used to transport imported paper (Ely and Deanside) and zinc (for Bloxwich) through the Port of Immingham.

Martin Buck

Petroleum Products : Back on familiar territory .... the first of two images sees No.60044 (above) on 15th May passing Barnetby 20 minutes into its six hour journey with 6M00, the 10:40 Kingsbury - Humber loaded petroleum tanks. Humber refinery sees much less traffic than Lindsey refinery.   **Mike Hemming**

No.60044 (below) crosses Todmorden Viaduct with the diverted 6E32, 10:21 Preston Docks - Lindsey empty bitumen tanks on 3rd February 2014, heading for Hall Royd Junction, where it will revert to its 'booked' route. The diversion was due to engineering work on the Copy Pit line, which involved the repair and strengthening of Holme Tunnel near the village of Holme Chapel.   **Neil Harvey**

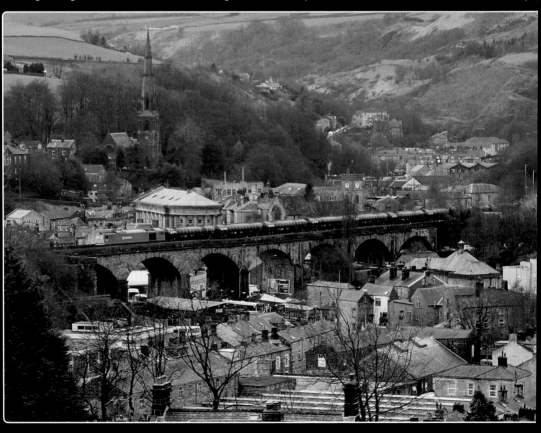

Steel : No.60044 (above) exits the loop at Sutton Bridge Junction, Shrewsbury, on 1st July with 6M76, the 00:38 Margam - Dee Marsh loaded steel. Whilst the main line is in shadow, due to 6M76 running 60 minutes late and ahead of 1W90 passenger, the train is held in the 'Up Goods Loop', which is fortunately bathed in sunshine. The Central Wales line can be seen deviating off to the right. **Mike Hemming**

Transrail Reminiscences .... **60066** *'John Logie Baird'* (above) in two-tone grey livery with Transrail logo and branding passes Slindon on the WCML with 6F38, the 17:19 (ThO) Sinfin - Stanlow empty aviation fuel tanks. The date is 6th May 1995 and this train has long-since ceased running. **Neil Harvey**

Here is another train made up of short wheel base wagons - 6E48, the 04:35 Stanlow - Jarrow loaded oil tanks - which is seen on 14th September 1996 passing through Hexham station with No.60066 'John Logie Baird' (below) in charge. This shot was taken on possibly the photographer's longest one day photographic trip - Oxfordshire to Hexham and back - over 600 miles in one day! **Martin Loader**

'Tug' Profile

60066

In Traffic
August 1991

Depot Allocation
August 1991	: Immingham
December 1991	: Toton
March 1994	: Cardiff
October 1996	: Toton

Livery
August 1991	: Two-Tone Grey
June 1996	: Transrail logo applied : White "T" in Blue circle with white and red borders.
?	: EWS 'Beasties' vinyl applied over Transrail branding
December 2013	: Silver livery with Drax Biomass branding.

Names
June 1991	: 'John Logie Baird'	*(nameplate carried on one side only)*

Withdrawn
: April 2006

Reinstated
: December 2013

(Above) : No.60066, bereft of nameplates, stands at Toton TMD on 3rd December 2013 unfinished, ready to receive 'powering tomorrow' and 'drax' branding. This is in association with the Drax Group's plans to be 'greener' and burn biomass instead of coal at Drax power station.   **Craig Adamson**

(Inset) : Theoretically stored at the time, No.60066 'John Logie Baird' heads past Slitting Mill Crossing on 5th April 2006 with 7E20, the 12:34 Toton - Doncaster Decoy departmental; EWS 'beasties' logo has been added to cover the 'Transrail' branding on the bodyside.   **Neil Harvey**

60066

The first image depicts the new look for No.60066 (above), complete with branding, as it approaches Whitley Bridge on 9th December 2013 with 6H84, the 10:46 Milford West Sidings - Drax PS biomass working; the smell of fresh paint was very strong as it passed!

Neil Harvey

Meanwhile, a blast from the past. Coal sector No.60066 'John Logie Baird' (above) crosses the River Leven viaduct with coal empties from Padiham power station (Burnley) to Maryport on 6th June 1992. Padiham received its last trainload of coal in 1993, ceasing power station generation on 31st March the same year.

Neil Harvey

Stone : On 23rd January, No.60066 (above) is seen passing Warmsworth, between Conisbrough and Doncaster, with a lightweight 6E51, the 12:21 Peak Forest - Selby loaded bogie hoppers. Although the train is only loaded to 10 bogies, there are four different types of hopper in the consist.

Ballast : The yellow 'IOA' Gondolas certainly add a splash of colour to proceedings, as No.60066 (below) heads 6M23, the 12:57 Doncaster VQ - Mountsorrel empty ballast on 10th February past Beighton. This train is routed via the Midland 'Old Road' to avoid Sheffield Midland station. **Alan Padley (2)**

Automotive : Class 60s are not regular performers on long distance automotive and wagonload services, so No.60066 turning up on 6M38, the 23:38 Southampton Eastern Docks - Halewood on 29th January is a real bonus. No.60066 (above) is seen passing through Eastleigh station, having previously come south overnight on the 6O42 loaded car train from Halewood.   **Simon Howard**

Metals : No.60066 (below) in Drax Biomass livery passes East Usk, Newport, with 6V75, the 09:30 Dee Marsh - Margam (via Llanwern) empty steel carriers on Thursday, 9th January. The train is loaded to 24 bogies and is a mix of wagon types: telescopic 'BYAs' and curtain-sided 'IHAs'.   **Chris Perkins**

60045
6N75

'On Manoeuvre'....

(Stage 1) ; An Eddie Stobart lorry heads north on the M1 Motorway, on 21st october 2013, as No.60045 'The Permanent Way Institution' (left) heads underneath and across the River Don with 6N75, the 15:33 (WFO) Aldwarke U.E.S. - Tees Dock Bsc Export Berth steel.

The consist is 2-axle 'SPA' Open Plate Wagons carrying steel wire and 'BDA'-type Bogie Bolster wagons housing steel rods.

This particular service runs south from Aldwarke to Tinsley Yard to run round, before heading back north.

Meanwhile, a little further on, No.60045 (opposite) is now running adjacent to the Sheffield 'Tram' system at Meadowhall South/Tinsley, with 6N75.

(Stage 2) : Having made the reversal at Tiinsley, No.60045 (below) is now heading back the way it came. The unelectrified line to the right is the freight line which runs from Tinsley East Jct. to Broughton Lane Jct., and is used by local steel 'trips' running between Aldwarke and Deepcar. **Alan Padley (3)**

Timings			
ALDWARKE	Dep.	15:33	16:59 - 17:04
Rotherham Central [RMC]	Pass	15:39	16:54
Tinsley East Junction	Pass	15:42	16:41
Tinsley South Junction		15:45 - 15:51	16:33 - 16:39
Shepcote Lane Junction	Pass	15:55	16:31
TINSLEY S.S.	Arr. / Dep.	15:59	16:27

Ratcliffe on Soar : This elevated view shows No.60017 (above) passing the giant cooling towers at Ratcliffe power station on 2nd May with 6E38, the 13:54 Colnbrook - Lindsey empty aviation fuel oil bogie tanks. East Midlands Parkway station is also visible on the right of shot.   **Jamie Squibbs**

Healey Mills : Yes, this is the once bustling Healey Mills marshalling yard. On 21st November 2013, Doncaster 'super shunter' No.60071 'Ribblehead Viaduct' (below) is sent to collect some of the redundant wagons that had been left abandoned when the yard was closed. The loco, still in EWS maroon & gold livery, is seen amidst the golden brown foliage, where it spent most of the day shunting wagons around the yard.   **Derek Holmes**

"50 Shades of Grey"

Tunstead : Silver-Grey Class 60, No.60099 (opposite), blends into the stark industrial surroundings, as it makes its way through the cement loading area at Tunstead on 25th September with 6H22 to Hindlow, having taken on its fill of limestone about half-a-mile further back. The limestone will be converted to form quicklime (Calcium Oxide) at Dowlow, and has many uses.   **David Hayes**

Seaforth : On 20th June, one of the few remaining 'tugs' still sporting the EWS maroon & gold livery, No.60035 (above), ambles down the Bootle Extension Line in Liverpool Docks. It is passing the Allied Mills grain silos, running light engine as 0E14, Tuebrook Sidings - Seaforth to collect empty steel carriers and return as 6E14, the 16:05 Seaforth - Tinsley.   **Colin Partington**

(Overleaf)
"Water, Water, Everywhere ...."

(Page 110)

Nether Lock Weir : The Nottingham to Lincoln railway crosses the River Trent at Nether Lock weir, Newark, where No.60100 (top) is seen on 14th May, heading 6E54, the 10:40 Kingsbury - Humber with the sugar beet factory in the background. The River Trent rises on Biddolph Moor, Staffordshire, and joins the River Ouse at Trent Falls. The two rivers combine to form the Humber Estuary.   **Alan Padley**

Northwich Viaduct : On 26th December 2013, No.60007 'The Spirit of John Kendell' (bottom) passes over the 1860-built viaduct with a rake of loaded 'JEAs', forming 6F05, the 15:19 (MWFO) Tunstead - Oakleigh, limestone heading for the Brunner Mond chemical works. This viaduct has 48 arches which span the River Weaver, Weaver Navigation, the A533 road and the River Dane. It is constructed in sandstone and brick, with iron girders crossing the River Weaver and Navigation.   **Colin Partington**

(Page 111)

Sawley Lock : 'Two Tugs for the Price of One' .... well, sort of! On 26th February, No.60092 (top) passes over the River Trent at Sawley Lock, where the tug boat 'Uranus' is moored. The train is 6E41, the 11:41 Westerleigh - Lindsey empty petroleum tanks and Sawley Lock is just south of Long Eaton, close to where the borders of Derbyshire, Leicestershire and Nottinghamshire meet.   **Alan Padley**

Fairburn Ings : Class 60s are not a regular sight on the 'freight-only' Castleford - Milford Junction line. On 22nd February, fresh from overhaul, No.60040 'The Territorial Army Centenary' (bottom) passes Fairburn Ings, Castleford, with a long rake of empty 2-axle open wagons, forming 7T51, the 10:40 Doncaster Up Decoy - Temple Hirst Junction. Fairburn Ings is a RSPB nature reserve and the word 'ings' is of Old Norse origin, meaning 'meadowland which floods'.   **Neil Harvey**

'Murco' Diversity

A little thought has gone into the composition of these two images ....

60092 (above) is seen passing under the cable stayed River Wye Bridge, which carries the M48 motorway, on 28th November 2013 with 6B13, the 05:00 Robeston - Westerleigh loaded Murco bogie tanks service at Thornwell, near Chepstow. In the background, the towers of the River Severn Suspension Bridge can be seen, which rise to 445 ft above mean high water.

Chris Davies

60040 'The Territorial Army Centenary' (below) emerges from the fog at Bourton on 1st July with the diverted 6A11, 22:49 Robeston - Theale loaded Murco oil tanks. The train was booked via Swindon, instead of its usual route via Newbury, and an early start was required for this 05:38hrs picture. The Met Office had forecast a sunny morning and only during the longest summer days can a picture be taken from the north side of the line at this spot. The photographer was not impressed to find the location in thick fog upon arrival. However, fortune favours the brave and, miraculously just before the train appeared, the sun broke through the fog, but only just in this one spot, which produces a very atmospheric picture - well worth getting up early for!

Martin Loader

60074 **Trent** : A different perspective at dusk, which captures the glint on the tanks to good effect. No.60074 'Teenage Spirit' (above) throws out a cloud of black smoke as the driver opens up from the speed restrictions at Trent with 6E59, the 15:41 Kingsbury - Lindsey Oil Refinery empty petroleum bogie tanks. The location is Meadow Lane Crossing, Trent; 27th March, at dusk and in the rain! **David Hayes**

West Drayton : On 12th March, No.60074 'Teenage Spirit' (below) is seen on 6E38, the 13:54 Colnbrook - Lindsey, waiting at West Drayton to join the Great Western Main Line. Colnbrook receives aviation fuel for Heathrow airport and the oil terminal is at the end of a three mile single line stretch of the former Staines & West Drayton Railway. Sadly, the distinct blue colour and Teenage Cancer Trust branding is no more, abandoned by DBS in September in favour of corporate red! **Guy Houston**

'BORDERLANDS'

Wrexham, Mold and Connahs Quay Line

The 13 mile stretch of line between Wrexham General and Shotton is seldom illustrated, despite some excellent photographic opportunities. This may be due to the fact there is little freight to observe in any given 24-hour period.

The current freight services are:

6M18, New Cumnock - Penyffordd

6M76, Margam - Dee Marsh

6V75, Dee Marsh - Margam

6M86, Margam - Dee Marsh

6V80, Dee Marsh - Margam

Coal is supplied to Castle Cement Works (6M18), conveyed in 'MEA' 2-Axle Open Wagons on a weekly service and can be sourced from Redcar.

The other four services listed are all steel related, linking the steelworks at Shotton (Dee Marsh) and Port Talbot (Margam); the latter, involving Class 60 traction, is featured here.

(Selective Images) :

(Above) :

Wrexham General : The front end of No.60039 (above) is glimpsed whilst waiting time at platform 3 for a path to leave Wrexham General station on 6th May with 6M86, the 09:23 Margam - Dee Marsh loaded steel. After Wrexham General, the 'tug' will proceed to Hawarden and Dee Marsh via Wrexham Exchange Junction.

(Overleaf, Page 116) :

Buckley : *"Here it comes"* .... some eight or so miles later, No.60039 (top) prepares to level out after climbing to Buckley with a heavy 6M86. The gradients from Shotton up to the summit at Buckley are more fearsome than from the Wrexham side with two long stretches of 1 in 53 either side of Hawarden. Penyffordd signal box is visible at the bottom of the incline. The milepost shows 8m. and 60ch., which is the mileage from Wrexham Central.

Cefn-y-bedd : No.60044 (bottom) passes Cefn-y-bedd on 1st July with 6V75, the 09:30 Dee Marsh - Margam, in a wooded area of the River Alyn valley, Flintshire, North East Wales. The location name translates into English as 'Behind the Grave.' This line is the former Wrexham, Mold and Connah's Quay Railway, which originated from Wrexham Exchange.

(Overleaf, Page 117) :

Penyfford : This shot dates back to 22nd April 2012, but is still relevant today to show the semaphore signals in use at Penyfford, No.60079 (top) approaches the station with 6M30, Margam - Dee Marsh loaded steel. The signal box at Penyffordd is the only signal box between Wrexham and Dee Marsh, controlling the station area and the siding leading to Castle Cement Works, which is about half a mile further north of here.

Shotton : On 2nd July, No.60020 (bottom) heads 6V80, the 20:39 Dee Marsh - Margam as it approaches Shotton station, looking back to Hawarden Bridge station on the other side of Hawarden Railway Bridge. The bridge was built by the Manchester, Sheffield and Lincolnshire Railway (which later became the Great Central Railway), opening on 3rd August 1889 and spans the River Dee.

Colin Partington (5)

The 'Aggregate' Score

No.60010 (above) hauls 6H60, the 15.25 Hope Street - Peak Forest stone empties on 6th June across Chapel Milton viaduct; a magnificent bifurcating railway viaduct. The 'tug' is on the section, built around 1867, which curves to the west whilst the other one, built in 1890, curves to the east.

This splendid view is looking south from the top of Peak Forest Tunnel. On 21st July, No.60074 'Teenage Spirit' (below) in Teenage Cancer Trust light blue livery turns into Wye Dale working 6H22, the 11.08 Tunstead - Hindlow limestone, Although a DBS operated service, it is formed of FHH bogie hoppers, which are interchanged with Buxton Lime Industries (BLI) wagons. **David Hayes (2)**

On a balmy late summer day, and almost catching the photographer by surprise, DBS Tug No.60001 (above) comes around the corner at Brierlow Bar on 16th September with 6H23, the 14:16 Hindlow (Briggs Sidings) - Tunstead empty BLI limestone hoppers, running 120 minutes early. In the foreground can be seen the remnants of the loading sidings at the long closed Buxton Quarry. **David Hayes**

'King of the Mountains' : On 2nd May, No.60079 (below) tackles the 1 in 200 gradient near Hathersage in the Hope Valley, working an additional 6E51, 12:21 Peak Forest - Selby loaded stone hoppers, comprising a mix of at least five different designs of bogie hopper. **Steven Brykajlo**

"Colas acquire 60s"

Background

Colas Rail, having already added new 'Powerhaul' Class 70s to their loco fleet, go one step further and announce (perhaps, surprisingly) the purchase of some Class 60s from DBS.

The deal was secured on 31st March with Colas acquiring the following 20 'tugs', interestingly the same 20 locos DBS put up for sale in September 2013. The first batch have been allocated to the 'COLS' Stored Loco Pool, while the second batch remain in the 'WQDA' (DBS Locomotives Stored Surplus Group 4) Pool at Crewe and Toton for the time being.

Number	Pool	Location	In Traffic	Fuel Capacity (Gallons)	
60002	COLS	Crewe DMD	1992	1,150	Extra Fuel Capacity
60021	COLS	Toton TMD	1990	1,150	
60026	COLS	Toton TMD	1990	1,150	
60047	COLS	Crewe DMD	1991	990	Normal Fuel Capacity
60056	COLS	Crewe DMD	1991	1,150	
60076	COLS	Crewe DMD	1991	990	
60085	COLS	Toton TMD	1991	990	
60087	COLS	Toton TMD	1991	990	
60095	COLS	Crewe DMD	1992	990	
60096	COLS	St. Blazey	1992	1,150	

'WQDA' Class 60s :

60013 / 60028 / 60029 / 60033 / 60038 / 60041 / 60046 / 60048 / 60055 / 60061

The First One

60087

Fresh from the paintshop, Colas Class 60 No.60087 (above) stands proud at Toton TMD on 30th May sporting its new colours, very reminiscent of the former Loadhaul orange & black livery which was so striking on 37s, 56s and 60s.

On Wednesday, 18th June, No.60087 is named 'CLIC Sargent' in recognition of the support provided by the charity to children suffering with cancer. A £15,000 cheque is also presented to the charity representative on behalf of Network Rail.

Craig Adamson

No.60087 'Slioch' (top right) is seen in **Two-Tone Grey Mainline** livery at Hither Green depot on 9th August 1997. It heads a line up of a 37, 08, two snowploughs, 31 and 33. A Class 47/3, No.47365 'Diamond Jubilee', is also in attendance. **Ian Cuthbertson**

60087 carried **EWS Maroon & Gold**, before conversion to Colas colours. On 21st December 2005, No.60087 (below) passes the time in between duties at Immingham TMD.

In April 2004, No.60087 received the name 'Barry Needham' (middle) off No.56115, in memory of the EWS coal train controller, who was tragically killed at Great Heck (ECML) on 28th February 2001.

On this fateful day 10 people died, including the drivers of both trains involved. The crash occurred when a Land Rover towing a loaded trailer swerved off the M62 motorway, ran down an embankment and onto the southbound railway track.

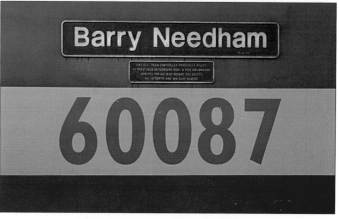

The Land Rover was hit by a southbound GNER InterCity 225 heading from Newcastle to London King's Cross, which was deflected into the path of FHH No.66521 heading an Immingham - Ferrybridge coal train. **Craig Adamson (2)**

60087 'In action' .... On 25th February 2000, No.60087 'Slioch' (above) negotiates New Mills South Junction with 6H60, 09:08 Hope Street - Peak Forest empties and passes the signal box which, at this time, had yet to be refurbished. The 60 is coming off the New Mills Central line, while the other lines lead to Stockport (via Hazel Grove Chord) and Northenden (via Hazel Grove High Level Junction). **Neil Harvey**

Alongside the banks of the River Severn, No.60087 'Barry Needham' (below) passes Gatcombe on 4th October 2005 with 6V05, the 09.29 Round Oak - Margam steel empties. Interestingly, No.60087 is the only Class 60 to have had its original name transferred to another class member, that being No.60069 'Humphrey Davy'. No.60087 was then subsequently named 'Barry Needham'. **Peter Slater**

A colourful array of Colas orange and yellow rolling stock sweeps into view at Old Linslade (WCML) on 4th July, as No.60087 'CLIC Sargent' + No.70804 (above) double head 6Z70, the 08:50 Rugby DED - Eastleigh East Yard crane move. Another Colas 70, No.70810, is 'DIT' on the rear of the train.   **Nigel Gibbs**

On 17th September, No.60087 'CLIC Sargent' (below) approaches Steventon with the late running 6V62, 11:12 Tilbury - Llanwern steel empties. They're gone, only three cooling towers remain, following demolition of the three southern cooling towers at Didcot A power station on 27th July. Soon, the view will change again when masts and catenary wires are erected for GWML electrification.   **Martin Buck**

66718

UK Arrival	April 2006
	Newport Docks
	MV 'Jumbo Challenger'
Built	EMD plant, London, Ontario, Canada
Initial Use	One of a dedicated fleet of five locos (66718 - 66722) to work engineer's trains under a 10-year, £80 million upgrade of London Underground network.

Livery	April 2006	: First GBRf 'Metronet' (Blue with Orange cabsides)
	November 2013	: London Underground 150 anniversary special livery

Names	January 2007	Gwyneth Dunwoody	London Euston station
	November 2013	Sir Peter Hendy CBE	London Victoria station

Notes	The new livery of No.66718 is all-over black colour with famous quotes on London, plus graphic representations of London's taxis, electric bus, cable car and 'S' stock.
	The loco was repainted by Arlington Fleet Services, Eastleigh.

66718 'Sir Peter Hendy OBE' (above) stabled at Felixstowe on 8th November 2013. **Michael Davies**

(Opposite) : No.66718 (top left) leads failed Class 20s No.20118 and No.20096 into Derby station on 14th January with 'S' Stock sets No.21049 and No.21050, forming 7X10, Amersham - Derby Litchurch Lane. Fellow Class 20s, No.20311 + No.20314, are on the rear. **Mick Tindall**

Here, No.66718 (middle) is illustrated powering towards the camera at Middle Road UWC, on the outskirts of March, leading a fully laden 4L02, the 03:55 Hams Hall - Felixstowe South Intermodal service. Reported as 114 minutes late at Oakham, the train is now about 30 minutes behind schedule, having missed out its booked 2½ hour layover at Peterborough. **James Welham**

Now, not looking quite so shiny, having spent four months on power station biomass and coal duties, No.66718 (bottom left) crawls out of Lynemouth power station on a sunny 28th February with 4N85, the 10:33 empty coal hoppers bound for Tyne Dock. **Martin Cook**

(Overleaf) : It certainly looks colourful, but the new colour scheme is somewhat confusing on the eye and it's difficult to make out the graphics. On 14th November 2013, No.66718 passes Earles Sidings in the Hope Valley with 6V09, the 14:14 Tunstead - Brentford loaded limestone. The consist is a rake of de-branded FHH 'JGA' Bogie Hoppers, 'Jolly Green Giants'. **Alan Padley**

66721

UK Arrival	April 2006	
	Newport Docks	
	MV 'Jumbo Challenger'	
Built	EMD plant, London, Ontario, Canada	
Initial Use	One of a dedicated fleet of five locos (66718 - 66722) to work engineer's trains under a 10-year, £80 million upgrade of London Underground network.	
Livery	April 2006	: First GBRf 'Metronet' (Blue with Orange cabsides)
	November 2013	: London Underground 150 anniversary special livery
Names	January 2007	Harry Beck	London Euston station

Notes   The livery of No.66721 has a different theme to that of No.66718. It is all-over white and carrying a section of the tube map. On one side is the cream-coloured 1933 version designed by Harry Beck, while on the other is the modern day 2013 version.

The loco was repainted by Arlington Fleet Services, Eastleigh.

November 2013 : No.66721 rededicated 'Harry Beck' at London Victoria station.

66721 'Harry Beck' : On 19th December 2013, No.66721 (above) cruises past the brick works and towards Ramsey Road crossing, Whittlesea, leading 6L76, the 07:24 Stud Farm - Whitemoor loaded ballast in 'IOA' wagons. The train is running around 50 minutes behind schedule having had an extended recess in Melton Mowbray Loop. The load of 20 'IOA' wagons weighs in at 2,032 tonnes. **James Welham**

(Opposite) : Oh dear, a not-so-resplendent, No.66721 (top) tries to blend in with its muddy surroundings at Northfleet Lafarge Terminal, when seen on 28th November 2013. It is waiting to depart with 6V93, the 11:10 Northfleet - Paddington Crossrail. In the background, the MV. 'Norsky' passes Tilbury container terminal, as it makes its way out to sea. This ship is a 'Ro-Ro' cargo ship, built in 1999 by Aker Finnyards, Finland, and has Rotterdam as its port of Registry. **Michael Davies**

In another elevated view, London Tube Map liveried Class 66/7 No.66721 (bottom) winds along the Fagbury link line out of Felixstowe North Terminal on 24th January with 4M23, the 10:46 Felixstowe - Hams Hall intermodal. The North terminal opened in June 2013. **Michael Davies**

(Previous Page) : On 27th January, No.66721 is seen heading 6M73 the 10:52 Doncaster - Toton departmental service at Hexthorpe Junction, about to join up with the lines on the left, which 'avoid' Doncaster station between here and Bentley Junction. The consist is a mix of 2-Axle Open Sided Wagons and 'JZA' Bogie Long Welded Rail Wagons. **Alan Padley**

1933   Harry Beck   **2013**

Thoresby Colliery Junction

Thoresby Colliery Junction is where the line to the colliery leaves the main line; the signal box here controls the run-round loop for the Thoresby Colliery Branch, plus the High Marnham Test Track.

This junction is now the limit of the 'freight only' line from Clipstone Junctions; coal trains ran for a further 10.50 miles east to High Marnham power station, until it closed in 2003 after 45 years of generation. The route from Thoresby to High Marnham remains in situ, now only used by Network Rail measurement trains and trains that trial new technology.

This line was once part of the Lancashire, Derbyshire and East Coast Railway, which arose out of a perceived need for an East-West line, the plan being to take it from Warrington on the Manchester Ship Canal to Sutton-on-Sea on the east coast of Lincolnshire. It was largely financed by a group of coal owners, led by William Arkwright, a descendant of Richard Arkwright.

The line from Chesterfield to Lincoln opened in 1897 but, unfortunately, this was to be the only part of the railway actually completed. The railway was bought by the Great Central Railway in 1907.

It has been announced that Thoresby Colliery will close in 2015.

Background

In 2012 and 2013, GBRf imported five General Motors Class 66s from Europe to complement their existing fleet of Class 66/7 locos.

Having received GBRf branding, albeit retaining their original livery, these locos are profiled in this issue of *LR 2015* to record their place in GBRf history.

No.	Arrived	From	Notes
66747	December 2012	Holland	Stored at Rossendaal
66748	December 2012	Holland	Stored at Rossendaal
66749	December 2012	Holland	Stored at Rossendaal
66750	June 2013	Germany	Ex-'Rush Rail'
66751	June 2013	Germany	Ex-'Rush Rail'

Where are they? - 2nd January

No.	Location	Working	Commodity
66747	Tyne Dock	6H37, 15:12 Tyne Dock - Drax	loaded biomass
66748	Doncaster		
66749	Drax	4N30, 15:12 Drax - Tyne Dock	empty biomass
66750	Newbiggin	4E13, 12:40 Newbiggin - Doncaster Decoy	empty gypsum
66751	Ironbridge		

66747 : The grey liveried Class 66/7 No.66747 (above) has now received GBRf branding and is seen on 23rd May passing Colton South Junction with 6H30, the 09:45 Tyne Dock - Drax loaded biomass, formed of new 'IIA' (UIC code Tafoos) Bogie Biomass Covered Hoppers. These colourful hoppers were introduced in 2013 and are suitably adorned with new '*drax*' and '*powering tomorrow*' branding. Drax is converting half of its firing capacity to use biomass fuels (wood pellets, primarily from Canada and the USA)) and has invested in a 200-strong fleet of purpose-built hoppers, designed and built in the UK.   **Ian Ball**

(Opposite) : 66748 sits in the run-round sidings at Thoresby Colliery Junction on 8th April, awaiting a crew change before proceeding to the colliery with 4K55, the 12:21 West Burton - Thoresby empty 'HYA' coal hoppers.   **Alan Padley**

66748

No.66748 (above) is seen on 14th May at Clipstone West Junction with 6B56, the 16:00 Thoresby - West Burton loaded coal. The train is about to pass a typical junction semaphore signal; the higher, left-hand arm (CJ43) applies to the main line and the right-hand arm (CJ37) serves the branch to Rufford.

Meanwhile, No.66748 (below) crosses the Chesterfield Canal on Manton Viaduct, Worksop, on 8th April with 4K55, the 12:21 West Burton - Thoresby empties. This well balanced view is framed by the overhang of the canal footbridge, looking through one of the eight arches of the railway viaduct to a more modern structure which leads across the water, which gives access from the B6079 Retford Road to Rayton Farm.

Alan Padley (2)

66749 (above) is seen passing the famous "EDINBURGH 200 MILES" sign at Shipton by Benningbrough on 16th April with 6H12, the 06:23 Tyne Dock - Drax loaded biomass. This train is formed of converted 'HYA' bogie hoppers, reclassified 'IIA', fitted with automated top doors to keep the biomass dry.   **Ian Ball**

66750 (below) passes Old Denaby, near Mexborough, on 12th May with a special 6Z56, Mountsorrel - Doncaster, formed of 'PHA' 2-Axle Hoppers, normally found in the Lafarge Self-Discharge Train. This line is the former South Yorkshire Railway, opening on 10th November 1849 between Swinton Junction and Doncaster, eventually absorbed by the Manchester, Sheffield and Lincolnshire Railway in 1864.   **Alan Padley**

66751 (above) is indicative of how the imported GBRf 66/7s are spreading their wings away from biomass and coal duties. On 1st July, No.66751 passes Bessacarr Junction with 4L78, the 12:00 Selby - Felixstowe intermodal. The train is coming off the single line spur from Decoy North Jct., while the main line to the left leads to Decoy South Jct.. No.66751 has since received GBRf/Europorte colours.

66747 (below) is seen here, around 18:30hrs, in the best lighting of an otherwise disappointing 19th April, approaching Milford with 6H98, the 15:37 Tyne Dock - Drax loaded biomass. The train is passing under the Leeds - Selby - Hull main line. **Alan Padley (2)**

Background History

January 2012 : Direct Rail Services (DRS) place an order for fifteen, 99mph, locos from Vossloh España in Valencia, Spain, to be delivered from late 2013. The contract is estimated to be worth £45 million and Vossloh have adapted its 'Eurolight' loco capable of operating within the UK loading gauge. DRS also have the option for a further 10 Class 68s (68016 - 68025), which they take up later in 2014.

The new locos have been classified under TOPS as Class 68.

Use

The Class 68 is a mixed-traffic loco intended for use on both passenger and freight trains and DRS plan to use the 68s on intermodal traffic and Network Rail departmental trains, but not nuclear flask trains.

Six Class 68s (Nos.68010 - 68015) will be sub-leased to Chiltern Railways to haul its entire fleet of Mark 3 vehicles, operating between London Marylebone - Birmingham / Kidderminster. The 68s will replace the current Class 67s and heavy maintenance will be undertaken by DRS.

Delivery

No.68001 spends most of 2014 being tested at Velim Test Centre in the Czech Republic prior to being made fit for delivery; No.68002 becomes ***the first 68 to arrive in the UK***.

68001	:	29th August, discharged off MV. 'Eendracht', at Liverpool Gladstone Dock.
68002	:	18th January, shipped from Bilbao to Southampton Eastern Docks.
68003 - 68005	:	15th April, discharged off the MV. 'Tasman' at Liverpool Gladstone Dock.
68006 - 68008	:	10th June, discharged off MV. 'Atlantic' at Liverpool Gladstone Dock.
68009 - 68011	:	31st July, discharged off MV. 'Deo Valente', at Liverpool Gladstone Dock.
68012 - 68014	:	29th August, discharged off MV. 'Eendracht', at Liverpool Gladstone Dock.

Courtesy Direct Rail Services

Names

The first nine Class 68s are named, broadly following a naval theme, like the British Rail Class 42s and 50s:

68001 'Evolution'
68002 'Intrepid'
68003 'Astute'
68004 'Rapid'
68005 'Defiant'
68006 'Daring'
68007 'Valiant'
68008 'Avenger'
68009 'Titan'

68001 (left) is seen, prior to receiving DRS livery, in a neutral livery while on test at Velim in the Czech Republic.

The presence of the orange box on the front, indicates it is fitted with electric train supply.

As the loco is rated at 3,800hp, it becomes the UK's most powerful diesel since the 4,000hp No.HS4000 'Kestrel', built in 1967.

'Early Arrivals'

68002 'Intrepid' becomes the first Vossloh Class 68 to run on the main line. Testing starts in February and four Riviera Trains coaches are sent to Carlisle on 4th February to be added to DRS' own Mk.2s to provide a rake with sufficient brake force for a high-speed test run on the WCML. At Carlisle, Class 90 No.90020 'Collingwood' + No.68002 + 11 Mk.2s is formed and the ensemble (above) is seen passing Euxton, running as 5Z69, the 11:02 Carlisle - Crewe. **Fred Kerr**

68001 Defiant', 68004 'Rapid' and 68003 'Astute' (below) are being towed through Earlstown on 16th April by DRS Class 37/6 No.37609, running as 0Z38, Liverpool Gladstone Dock - Crewe Gresty Bridge. The 37 is leaving Earlstown West Jct. to join the WCML at Earlstown South Jct. **Simon Howard**

OFFLOADING

68003 'Astute' (above) is seen on 15th April in the process of being lifted out of the hold and onto the quayside at Liverpool's Gladstone Dock steel terminal from the MV. 'TASMAN'. This is a small general cargo vessel with a gross tonnage of 2,999 tons, built in 2007 by Ferus Smit Scheepswerf, Hoogezand in the Netherlands, sailing under a Gibraltar flag.

68009 'Titan' (below) and Nos.68010 and 68011, the latter two locos being the first to be delivered in a livery of two shades of grey (Chiltern Railways), stand on the quayside at Liverpool's steel terminal on 31st July. The locos have been offloaded from the Dutch registered cargo vessel MV. 'DEO VALENTE' and are coupled up to DRS Class 57 No.57012, which will take the three new locos to Crewe.   **Philip Parker (2)**

68004
'Rapid'

1st Revenue Earning Run

68004 'Rapid' (right) is seen on a dull and wet 28th May heading south at Hanch, near Lichfield TV (WCML) towing loaded 'JNA' 'Falcon' Bogie Ballast Wagons.

It's the first 'earner' for the new Class 68 and the train is 6Z76, Crewe Basford Hall - Willesden. Fellow DRS locos Class 47 No.47805 + Class 66 No.66426 are tucked inside as insurance.

John Whitehouse

The loco has been busy since entering service moving On Track Plant vehicles and pasenger rolling stock to and from East Anglia.

A lightweight ECS move ensues for No.68004 'Rapid' (middle) on 20th August, when it is seen passing Chelmscote on the WCML with a Greater Anglia Mk3 in tow. The train is running as 5Z68, the 12:21 Wolverton Centre Sidings - Norwich Crown Point.

On 4th August, No.68004 'Rapid' (bottom right) makes a first appearance for the Class at March, when it approaches March East Junction level crossing with 6Z12, the 13:48 Stowmarket - Whitemoor MPV move.

It seems quite appropriate for a loco with a product name of 'UKLIGHT' (derived from Vossloh, 'Eurolight') to haul such a light load!

Nigel Gibbs (2)

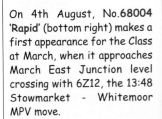

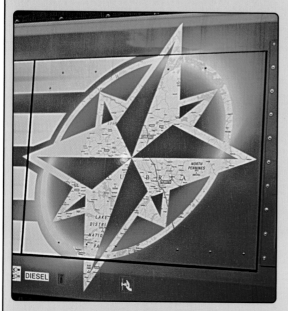

DRS
Crewe Gresty Bridge Open Day

19th July

At the annual DRS 'Open Day', along with other DRS locos on display to the public, five of their new Class 68 fleet are present:

68002

68004

68006

68007

68008

'Compass' Branding

A variation of the 'Flying Compass' is applied to each side of the new Class 68s.

All points of the compass radiate away from its centre, which is Carlisle, HQ of DRS.

All images : **Mark Thomas**

'On Display'

68002 'Intrepid' (above) stands in the depot yard at Crewe, Gresty Bridge, on a rather dull day with Class 47 No.47841 visible in the background. On the left is a 'heritage' DRS loco which displays the 'old' Compass branding, the new version of which is altogether more modern and striking in appearance.

68008 'Avenger' (below) inside the depot at Gresty Bridge. **Michael Wright (2)**

Direct Rail Services new Class 68 locos seem to be gradually filtering into revenue earning work after resolving a few teething problems. On 20th August, No.**68002** **'Intrepid'**(above) is entrusted with the daily Crewe - Mountsorrel working and is seen passing Hademore, near Lichfield, with the outward empties, 6U76 0859 ex-Crewe Basford Hall.

The tower of hay, constructed in the manner of an Egyptian step pyramid, presents an interest aside. Note, too, that the leaves on the foreground bushes are beginning to show the first hint of the onset of autumn. This viewpoint is from a new bridge which was constructed across the Trent Valley when it was 'four tracked' a few years ago. It replaced a level crossing, about 300 yards to the south.   **John Whitehouse**

Shap Ballast

On 2nd September, the new DRS Class 68 No.**68007 'Valiant'** is allocated to work 6C27 / 6C28 Shap Quarry ballast 'trip'. On the outward leg, No.68007 (above) is first seen heading south at Scout Green on the 1 in 75 descent to Tebay with 6C27, the 09:42 Carlisle VQ - Shap Quarry ballast empties, formed of Network Rail 'MRA' Bogie Side Tipping Ballast Wagons.

At Tebay, the 6C27 reverses (11:00 - 11:45hrs) and retraces its steps, as access to the quarry can only be gained from the 'Down Main' line. No.68007 (below) is now seen climbing past Greenholme heading to the quarry, from where the train can run direct to Carlisle without any further reversal. **Keith McGovern (2)**

'Shades of Grey'

68011 (left) makes a debut for the Class on 27th August along the North Wales Coast. It sits at Chester railway station on its way back to Crewe, while the driver and second man stretch their legs for 10 minutes, awaiting a path.

The driver training run went as far as Llandudno Junction on the outward run, but the 68 could not go beyond Bangor as the Class has not been cleared to go across the Britannia bridge into Anglesey. **Chris Williams**

Class 68 Specifications

Configuration	:	Bo-Bo
Length	:	66ft ins
Height	:	13ft .ins
Weight	:	85 tonnes
Diesel Engine	:	Caterpillar Inc. C175
Traction Motors	:	Four ABB 4FRA6063, frame mounted
Power Output	:	3,800 bhoy
Top Speed	:	99mph
Tractive Effort	:	71,000 lb (starting)
Fuel Capacity	:	1,100 gallons

68011 : The running-in process for the new Class 68s continues, with 6U76, 0859 Crewe Basford Hall - Mountsorrel empty ballast boxes and 6U77, the 13:42hrs loaded return, becoming a favoured train in which to test the locos. On 26th August, DRS turn out one of their 'Chiltern' liveried Class 68s, No.68011 (below), which is seen heading the loaded train alongside Lichfield Trent Valley Junction signal box, about to take the chord leading to the WCML Trent Valley route. **John Whitehouse**

68010 + 68011 make their main line debut on 20th August, running light engine as 0Z68, the 05:45 Crewe CLS - Carlisle Kingmoor. On the return journey, the Chiltern Railways liveried Nos.68010 and 68011 (above) head south through Acton Bridge in fading light, having collected seven Mk2s. **Chris Williams**

68011 : Having earlier worked 5Z55, 08:04 Norwich Crown Point - Wolverton, taking two Greater Anglia Mk.3 coaches for refurbishment, No.68011 returns on 5Z56, the 12:21hrs from Wolverton to Norwich Crown Point with newly refurbished coaches, Nos.12129 and 12147. No.68011 (above) is approaching Cheddington Station on Monday, 8th September, running six minutes behind schedule. **Geoff Plumb**

DRS Intermodal

4D47, Inverness - Mossend

68005 'Defiant' (above) becomes the first Class 68 to work a revenue-earning service North of the Border. It is seen passing Dalguise, near Dunkeld and Birnham, on the Highland Line, on 29th July hauling 4D47, the 13:19 Inverness - Mossend intermodal. No.68005 had earlier worked north on 4H47.   **Alastair Blackwood**

Perhaps, surprisingly, No.**68014** (below) becomes the first Chiltern liveried Class 68 to work in Scotland and on 23rd September it is seen waiting time alongside Platform 4 at Perth, whilst working 4D47 intermodal from Inverness to Mossend. This train is actually scheduled to wait at Perth two minutes at Platform 7, which is the farthest platform on the left.   **Jim Ramsay**

Here is another view of No.68014 (above) working 4D47, this time 'under the wires' passing Heatherbell level crossing on the Greenhill Lower Junction - Cumbernauld - Coatbridge - Mossend Yard - Motherwell main line. The northern limit of West Coast Main Line electrification is just north of here, between Garnqueen North Junction and Gartsherrie South Junction.   **Alastair Blackwood**

No.68005 'Defiant' (below) crosses Greenhill Lower Junction on 9th August, while working 4D47 intermodal, just as the sun starts to emerge from behind the darkest cloud in the sky, casting sunlight on the front half of the train. The line partially visible to the right of the loco leads to Greenhill Junction on the Glasgow Queen Street - Polmont - Edinburgh Waverley main line.   **Steven Brykajlo**

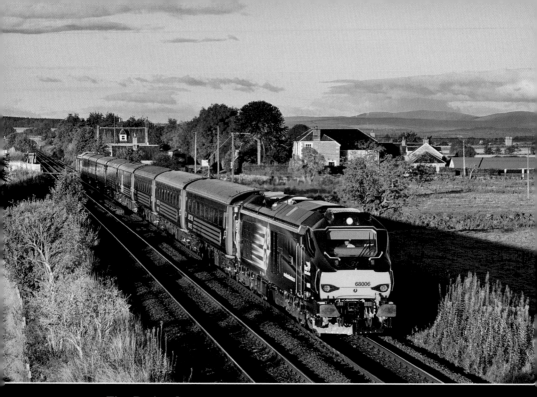

The Ryder Cup

Europe 16.5 pts   USA 11.5 pts

Fantastic golf and team Europe retain the Ryder Cup with Welshman Jamie Donaldson winning his match to win the Cup. With up to 50,000 spectators visiting the Centenary Course at Gleneagles each day, special loco-hauled trains are laid on to take spectators to and from the course.

Featured locos include DRS 57s, DBS 67s and, of particular interest, two of the new DRS Class 68s. Due to timings, it's the ECS workings which attract most attention.

Sample Diagram :

1Z25, 06:23 Glasgow Central - Gleneagles
5Z25, 07:46 Gleneagles - Dundee West Sidings
5Z56, 17:19 Dundee West - Gleneagles
1Z56, 18:29 Gleneagles - Glasgow Central

Locos :
Nos.**68005** and **68006** in top 'n' tail mode

(Above) : On 23rd September, the first day of Ryder Cup duties, No.68006 'Daring' and No.68005 'Defiant' shunt the stock off 1Z25 in Dundee West Sidings, whilst running as 5Z25, the 07:46 Gleneagles - Dundee West. The track in the foreground climbs to the Tay Bridge and the main line to Edinburgh. **Guy Houston**

(Top Left) : On 24th September, just after sunrise, No.68006 'Daring' gallops north with 5Z25, the 07:46 Gleneagles - Dundee West ECS, off the 1Z25, the 06:23 Glasgow Central - Gleneagles Ryder Cup "Golfex" at Forteviot, just south of Perth. No.68005 'Defiant' is on the rear. **Guy Houston**

(Bottom Left) : On Saturday, 27th September, No.68006 'Daring' leads 5Z16, the 08:17 Gleneagles - Polmadie ECS 'under the wires' at Greenfoot. The stock will be stabled and serviced at Polmadie before returning to Gleneagles to form 1Z59, the 18:49hrs service to Perth. **Alastair Blackwood**

(Below) : As the light begins to fade, No.68005 'Defiant' is seen skirting Invergowrie Bay with 5Z56, the 17:19 Dundee West - Gleneagles ECS on 23rd September - sister loco No.68006 'Daring' tails. Although the competition proper does not start until Friday, 26th September, extra trains are laid on beforehand for spectators wishing to attend the 'Pro-am' and practice rounds. **Jim Ramsay**

Class 68 'Trivia'

Names of Royal Naval Vessels since 1900

68001 'Evolution' : No naval connection - DRS refer to their 5 year corporate plan as 'Evolution'.

HMS Intrepid

1936 : 'I' Class Destroyer (D10) : Sunk by air attack in 1943.

1964 : 'Fearless' Class Landing Platform Dock : Laid up in 1991 and used for spare parts; scrapped in 2008.

HMS Astute

1944 : Amphion-Class Submarine (P447) : Keel laid down at Barrow-in-Furness and commissioned in 1945.
Part of the Fleet Review to celebrate the Coronation of Queen Elizabeth II, scrapped in October 1970.

2007 : Attack Submarine : Commissioned on 27 August 2010, when assigned her HMS prefix.
Largest attack submarine commissioned by the Royal Navy. Lead ship of her Class.
'Astute' is the second submarine to be named after the characteristic of shrewdness and discernment.

HMS Rapid

1916 : 'M' Class Destroyer : Sold in 1927.

1942 : 'R' Class Destroyer : Converted into a Frigate in 1952 and was sunk as a target in 1981.

68005 'Defiant' : No naval connection.

HMS Daring

1914 : 'L' Class Destroyer : Renamed 'Lance' in 1913, a year before launch.

1932 : 'D' Class Destroyer (H16) : Sunk in 1940.

1949 : Daring-Class Destroyer (D05) : Broken up in 1971.

2006 : Type 45 or 'Daring' Class Air Defence Destroyer.
Her name, crest and motto refer to the Roman youth Gaius Mucius Scaevola, famed for his bravery.

HMS Valiant

1914 : Queen Elizabeth-Class Battleship : Served in World War I and World War II. Sold for scrap in 1948.

1963 : Nuclear Powered Submarine (S102) : Lead boat of her Class. She was paid off in 1994.

HMS Avenger

1915 : Armed Merchant Cruiser : Torpedoed and sunk on 14 June 1917 by SM U-69.

1940 : Avenger-Class Aircraft Carrier (D14) : Converted from the merchant vessel 'Rio Hudson'.
She was transferred to the Royal Navy under lend-lease and was sunk by U-155 in 1942.

1945 : Landing Ship, 'Tank' : Launched in 1945 as LST 3011. She was renamed HMS Avenger in 1947.
Sold to the Royal Indian Navy in 1949 and renamed 'Magar' in 1951.

1975 : Type 21 Frigate (F185) : Fought in the Falklands War. Sold to Pakistan in 1994, renamed 'Tippu Sultan'.

HMS Titan

1935 : Armed Yacht : Requisitioned by the Admiralty in September 1939.
Served as Harbour Defence Patrol Craft.

(Launch year for each vessel shown)

BR Diesel Locos to carry a 'Warship' name :

Name	Class	Number	In Traffic	Withdrawn	
'Intrepid'	42	D825	August 1960	August 1972	
'Rapid'	43	D838	October 1960	March 1971	
'Daring'	42	D811	October 1959	January 1972	
'Valiant'	50	50015	April 1968	June 1992	(Preserved)
'Avenger'	42	D804	April 1959	October 1971	
'Titan'	47	D1665	March 1965		
		47080			
		47612		October 1999	(as 47779 unnamed)

"'Shape of Things To Come"

68002 'Intrepid' (right) make the first working for the Class along the Chiltern main line on 5th August, for crew training.

No.68002 stands at Princes Risborough as Class 67 No.67014 'Thomas Telford' speeds by with 1R22, the 10:15 London Marylebone - Birmingham Moor Street. From December 2014, the incumbent Class 67s will be replaced by Class 68s.

Geoff Plumb

68007 'Valiant' (above) passes through Kirkby Stephen on 3rd September with 0Z37, Preston - Carlisle Kingmoor crew training run and so makes the Class' debut on the Settle - Carlisle line; the loco earlier worked light engine (0Z36) from Carlisle to Preston. We will have to wait and see what duties, if any, the DRS 68s will perform over this famous line.   **Keith McGovern**

68009 'Titan' (above) passes Burton Salmon on 10th September with 6Z50, the 10:15 York Thrall - Stowmarket taking 'FEA' 60ft Flat Wagons housing modules for the autumn leaf clearing programme in East Anglia. These 'FEAs', usually two per train, hold Sandite, water tanks and jetting equipment.

Neil Harvey

A dazzling study of yellow and orange on 24th March, as No.70804 (above) heads past Compton Beauchamp on the GWML with another 6M50 going to Bescot, consisting on this occasion of the High Output Ballast Cleaner. Since their inception, the Colas 70s have made the 6V46 / 6M50 diagram their own. **Martin Loader**

70801

A reminder ....

No.70099 (left) arrives at the Brush factory, Loughborough, on 23rd October 2012 to enable rectification work to be carried out. It was towed there by FHH Class 66/5 No.66504 on a delayed 0Z62, the 10:14 Crewe Basford Hall - Loughborough.

At the time, it was not known where this loco was destined; perhaps, a replacement for FHH Class 70 No.70012, but no, the rumour mill always favoured Colas, and so it proved! **Jamie Squibbs**

UK Arrivals

Except for No.70801, the Colas Class 70s arrive in the UK via Seaforth, Liverpool, after being moved by rail from GE Transportation's plant in Pennsylvania to Norfolk, Virginia, for shipping across the Atlantic.

Date	No(s).		Ship
16th October 2012	70801		MV 'Sudkap'
4th January 2014	70803	70805	MV 'Atlantic Concert'
30th January	70804		MV 'Atlantic Compass'
28th February	70802		MV 'Atlantic Companion'
23rd April	70606	70807	MV 'Atlantic Concert'
17th May	70808	70809	MV 'Atlantic Compass'
26th May	70810		MV 'Atlantic Concert'

On 30th April 2013, No.70099 moves back to Crewe for tyre turning amongst other things, where it stays until June.

On 5th June, No.70099 (below) is moved to Eastleigh, via 4011, 00:23 Crewe Basford Hall - Southampton freightliner, DIT behind Class 66/5 No.66516 and is seen upon arrival at the Maritime terminal. **Simon Howard**

Background History

November 2013 : French-owned Colas Rail and GE Transportation announce an order for 10 Class 70 'PowerHaul' locos.

The Prototype

In February 2011, a dark green loco is unveiled at Eskisehir in Turkey, the product of a collaboration between General Electric and Tülomsas - No.DE 37001.

This ex-demonstration loco is tested by Turkish Railways and remains in Turkey until October 2012, when it is shipped to the UK, via Newport Docks.

The loco is assigned a temporary number, **70099** - and it is moved to Brush Traction in Loughborough, where it remains until the end of March 2013, so adjustments could be made to make it compatible for the UK's railway system. No.70099 also supplies parts for Freightliner Class 70s, No.70014 and No.70018, both locos being out of service at the time.

In December 2013, No.70099 is handed over to Colas Rail, as No.70801.

'Grime & Shine' : A work-worn Colas Class 66/8 No.66850 is seen towing No.70801 (above) through Eastleigh on 14th February, running as 0Z66, Cardiff Canton - Eastleigh. The 70 has received Colas colours and will now be involved in driver training, after which it will take up the same duties as the other Class members, departmental 'trips' out of Eastleigh and Westbury. **Simon Howard**

After much delay, No.70801 finally enters traffic. On 17th February, the ex-Turkish demonstrator makes its first run under its own power. With No.56302 as back up, No.70801 (top right) approaches Dilton Marsh Halt, running as 0Z70, the 10:12 Eastleigh - Westbury Yard. At Westbury, the 'grid' is exchanged for Nos.56094 + 56113, for a run back to Eastleigh via Bristol Barton Hill. **Mark Pike**

No.70801 runs light on 26th February to Acton Yard, from where it pilots 6V62, the 11:12 Tilbury - Llanwern. No.70801 + No.56078 (above) passes through the railway cutting at Purley on Thames with 6V62, formed of 'BYAs' and 'IHA' steel carriers. **Simon Howard**

On 18th April, we witness the first northbound run of a Class 70/8 over the Chiltern line. The doyen member of the fleet, No.70801 (below), approaches Princes Risborough five minutes early with 6C20, the 07:30 Southall East Junction - Hinksey Yard, with a trainload of old track panels. **Geoff Plumb**

On 11th March, Nos.70802 + 70805 are allocated to work 6M50, the 07:55 Westbury - Bescot, which are seen leaving Westbury Yard (above) and then passing Water Orton foot crossing (below), some seven hours and 145 miles later - a stunning sight. **Mark Pike / David Hayes**

On Tuesday, 18th March, Nos. 70802 (leading) + 70803 (rear) enter Dawlish Warren 'Down Loop' (above) with a ballast train from Westbury. The material is destined for Dawlish, where some 250 feet of track was damaged after sea wall foundations fell into the sea, following horrendous storms in late January and early February. This is the first Class 70 to visit Devon. **Robert Sherwood**

70803 (above) passes Milton, Didcot, on 10th March, slowing to take the curve from Foxhall Junction to Didcot North Junction with a payload of mostly Network Rail 'JNA' and DBS 'MLA' Bogie Ballast Wagons. This shot would not be ideal if the sun was shining, as the train would cast a shadow. The motor vehicles in view are heading down Milton Road, which leads from the A4130 to Milton Business Park. **Mark Pike**

On Thursday, 14th August, Colas Class 70 No.70804 becomes the first member of the Class to visit the North East of England, passing through Yorkshire, Durham and Northumberland.

This loco is moving a section of the High Output Ballast System and runs north via the GWML, London and then the ECML.

The return leg takes the more direct route via Birmingham. On 15th August No.70804 (right) is seen passing Burton Salmon on the 'Up Pontefract' main line with 6Z47, the 11:10 Tyne Yard - Cardiff Canton HOBS move.

6Z27, CARDIFF CANTON - TYNE YARD	14th August
6Z47, TYNE YARD - CARDIFF CANTON	15th August

70804

70804 (above) passes Milepost 158, Arksey foot crossing, two miles out of Doncaster on 14th August with 6Z27, the 06:16 Cardiff Canton - Tyne Yard HOBS working. This section of the ECML runs for 27 miles as double track from Doncaster to Colton Junction and, until the Selby Diversion opened in 1983, the train would have been routed via Selby and its famous swing bridge across the River Ouse. **Alan Padley (2)**

70805

At 23:40hrs on Wednesday, 7th May, No.70805 (above) comes into Platform 2 at Princes Risborough station with 6C31, the 20:25 Bescot - Claydon L&NE Junction with a Kirow crane and wagons of concrete sleepers for upgrade work on the Bicester to Oxford line. The train reverses here and departs for Aylesbury around 28 minutes late and becomes the first Class 70 to visit the County town of Buckinghamshire.   **Geoff Plumb**
On 14th April, No.70805 (below) sits at the rear of a ballast train at Bremhill Bridge, Swindon, on the recently doubled track between Swindon and Kemble, adjacent to the site of an emergency fuel bunker for RAF Lyneham. No.70803 (out of view) will lead the empty autoballasters into Swindon.   **Steven King**

70805 (above) passes through King's Sutton with 6M50, on time, on a rather dull 6th March. The last flood water can be seen to the right of the train, plus the 198ft high steeple of the Church of England parish church of Saints Peter and Paul, which dominates the skyline, and dates back to Norman times.   **Geoff Plumb**

Under a milky sky on 2nd July, No.70805 (below) rattles 10 autoballasters (2 x 5 wagon sets) across the A10 level crossing at Foxton, running as 6L37, the 09:58 Hoo Junction - Whitemoor. Foxton is on the line to Cambridge, which runs from Cambridge Junction (Hitchin) and joins the former Great Northern Line at Shepreth Branch Junction, just over two miles south of Cambridge.   **Nigel Gibbs**

70806 On 4th July, No.70806 (above) passes Fleet with 6Y41, the 09:02 Eastleigh Yard - Hoo Junction engineer's train, which is the return working of 6Y41, 09:02 Eastleigh - Hoo Junction. The consist is a train of Continuous Welded Rail Wagons (code 'YEA') with two 'Porpoise' Chute wagons behind the loco. The vantage point for this shot is a new multi-storey car park.   **Mark Pike**

(Opposite) : No.70806 + 70807 prepare to leave Liverpool Docks on 1st May, seen at Regent Road about to run light engine to Bescot to work 6V46, the 19:00 Bescot VQ - Westbury VQ service.   **Martin Williams**

A contrast of new and old .... a new No.70806 (below) is seen passing Bygrave (between Hitchin and Cambridge) on 29th May with 6L37, the 09:58 Hoo Junction- Whitemoor. The consist is four loaded 'Sea Cows', built between 1971 and 1982 at BREL Ashford and Shildon. This route was electrified as part of the Great Northern Route electrification programme in the mid 1970's, initially as far as Royston, before being extended to Cambridge in the 1980s.   **Nigel Gibbs**

"Land Ahoy"

The Colas Class 70s (Nos.70802 to 70810) arrive in the UK at Seaforth in the hold of an Atlantic Container Line 'ConRo' vessel. Each loco is housed on an ACL specialist Mafi trailer for easy loading and unloading.

On 23rd April, No.70807 is seen in the hold of the ship (above) on a trailer and then being offloaded (below) onto the quayside at Liverpool's Royal Seaforth Container Terminal. Nos. 70803, 70805 and 70810 are also shipped to the UK aboard the MV. 'Atlantic Concert'.

ACL (Atlantic Container Line) ship the Colas Class 70s across the Atlantic Ocean, using their fleet of 'ConRo' vessels; these stow containers on deck and have over 8,000ft available below deck for rolling cargo. One such example is the MV. 'Atlantic Companion' (above) seen berthed at Seaforth, which brought in Colas Class 70 No.70802. Nos.70804, 70808 and 70809 arrived on the MV. 'Atlantic Compass'.

Seaforth Dock : This aerial view shows Seaforth Dock, which is linked to Liverpool's Gladstone Dock and access to the River Mersey via a lock entrance (not in view). Here, MV. 'Atlantic Companion' (below) is seen berthed alongside a quayside packed with containers. The railway line can be seen on the left of shot, which carries biomass (Ironbridge ps), freightliner (Crewe/Coatbridge) and steel (Tinsley). **Philip Parker (4)**

70807

No.70807 (left) is seen stabled at Eastleigh on 11th May, awaiting its next turn of duty.   **Richard A. Jones**

On 20th May, No.70807 (below) heads a lengthy 6M50, the 07:55 Westbury - Bescot through Coventry station; the rear of which can still be seen coming off the Leamington line at Coventry South Junction.   **Mike Hemming**

Officially, this service is timed for 60mph maximum speed and a trailing load of 2,200 tonnes. The route taken by 6M50 is as follows:

Westbury 'Down' Traffic Centre
Melksham
Chippenham
Swindon
Foxhall Junction
Oxford
Leamington
Coventry
Nuneaton
Water Orton
Park Lane Junction
Walsall
Bescot 'Up' Engineers Sidings

Class 70 Specifications		
Configuration	:	Co-Co
Length	:	71ft 2.7ins
Height	:	12ft 10.2ins
Weight	:	129 tonnes
Diesel Engine	:	GE Powerhaul P616
Traction Motors	:	GE 5GEB30, Axle Hung
Power Output	:	3,690 bhp
Top Speed	:	75mph
Tractive Effort	:	120,000 lbf (starting)
Fuel Capacity	:	1,300 gallons

6C65 On 15th / 16th May, No.70807 plus No.70804 reach Penzance and undertake ballasting duties on the St. Ives branch, so becoming the first Colas 70s to reach the Royal Duchy of Cornwall.

In this view, No.70807 (above) leads 6C65, the 17:24 Westbury - St Erth past Langford Bridge, powering away from Aller Junction on the three mile climb to Dainton Summit. Construction is well underway on the A380 South Devon Link Road (Kingskerswell Bypass), which comprises a three mile dual carriageway road between Penn Inn (Newton Abbot) and the Torbay Ring Road at Kerswell Gardens.   **Robert Sherwood**

On the return journey, Nos.70807 + 70804 (below) top 'n' tail the empty autoballasters, seen alongside the M4 Motorway at Pugham Crossing, near Tiverton Parkway. The railway line actually runs for some 10 miles shadowing the course of the motorway between the villages of Burlescombe and Hele. No.70807 is the loco on the left of the consist.   **Peter Slater**

'ON HIRE'
to
FREIGHTLINER

Week commencing 26th May, Colas Rail come to the assistance of Freightliner and place two of their new Class 70s at their disposal to cover a loco shortage; Nos.70808 and 70805.

The following week, it's back to normal and Nos.70808 / 70805 are working departmental duties off Eastleigh and Westbury. This brief hire period is repeated again in August when No.70803 has a spell working freightliner trains between Southampton, Cardiff Wentloog and Leeds.

(Selective Images) :

On 29th May, No.70808 (right) is seen leaving the stabling point on the west side of Ipswich station, about to run light engine to Felixstowe, where it will work 4M92, the 18:13hrs departure to Lawley Street.

No.70808 arrived in the UK on 18th May and was offloaded from the ACL 'ConRo' vessel MV. 'Atlantic Compass' at Seaforth Dock, Liverpool. **Mark Pike**

70808

Along with No.70808 (top left), No.70805 is also out on short term hire to Freightliner, seen here at Felixstowe North terminal on 29th May in the company of GBRf Class 66/7 No.66731 'InterhubGB'. The locos scheduled departures are:

    70808 : 4R97, 09:12 Tilbury
    70805 : 4M88 09:32 Crewe Basford Hall
    66731 : 4M23, 10:46 Hams Hall

On 28th May, No.70808 (bottom left) is seen on the 'North' terminal traverser, going for a ride from track 2 to track 8, in order to head 4M93, the 13:30 service to Lawley Street. This new terminal opened on 6th June 2013, when the old 'North' terminal became the 'Central' terminal. **Michael Davies (2)**

There's no rest for the wicked .... after working 4M93 into Lawley Street, No.70808 (below) is despatched to the south coast with 4O18, the 03:50 Lawley Street - Southampton freightliner, which is seen on a rather dull 29th May passing Worting Junction, Basingstoke. **Simon Howard**

70809

A close up view of the final member of the first batch of 10 Colas Rail Class 70s ....

.... No.70810 (right) is stabled at Seaforth, Liverpool, on 29th May, having been unloaded off the MV 'Atlantic Concert'.

It will be a further five days before this latest member of the Colas Class 70 fleet leaves Seaforth to work its first revenue earning service in traffic (see below).

Chris Williams

70810

.... and here it is on its first day in traffic. No.70810 (above) pulls away from Worcester Shrub Hill station on 3rd June with 6Z70, the 14:38 Bescot Up Engineers Sidings - Long Marston, formed of four sets of 'MRA' Side Tipping Wagons loaded with spoil. Earlier the Colas 70 had worked light engine to Bescot. The loco is passing Milepost 120, which is the mileage from London Paddington via Didcot station, Oxford, Moreton in Marsh and Evesham.

Martin Jones

------ ~ ------

(Opposite) : On 23rd May, a day after entering service, No.70809 (top) hauls a rake of 'SSA' 2-Axle Scrap Wagons, while on hire to Freightliner. It is passing under the M1 Motorway at Moorbridge Lane, Stanton Gate, working 6M46, the 12:54 (MFO) Aldwarke - Crewe Basford Hall.

Neil Downing

No.70809 (bottom) heads away from Bexley with the daily 6Y41, 09:02 Eastleigh Yard - Hoo Junction departmental 'trip', photographed from the A2 road bridge which crosses the Lewisham - Dartford main line at this point. The steeple of St. John's parish church punctuates the treeline.

Stuart Chapman

State of Play

3rd June : All 10 Colas Rail Class 70s in Traffic

No.	Pool	Location	Allocated
70801	COLO	Eastleigh	
70802	COLO	Westbury	
70803	COLO	Eastleigh	
70804	COLO	Westbury	0M50, Westbury - Bescot
70805	COLO	Hinksey	0M50, Westbury - Bescot
70806	COLO	Hoo Junction	6L37, Hoo Junction - Whitemoor
70807	COLO	Eastleigh	
70808	COLO	Hinksey	0M50, Westbury - Bescot
70809	COLO	Hackney Yard	0Z29, Hackney Yard - Westbury
70810	COLO	Bescot	6Z70, Bescot - Long Marston

Colas Class 70 Miscellany

70801 + 70807 + 70806 (left) are seen entering Eastleigh station on 2nd May with 6Z30, the 17:26 Westbury - Eastleigh departmental 'trip'.

70802 + 70803 + 70805, can also be seen stabled; almost a full set at the time, only '804 missing! **Simon Howard**

On a rather hazy 17th April, Colas Class 66/8 No.66846 (below) passes Bourton, east of Swindon, with the daily 6M50, Westbury VQ - Bescot VQ 'trip'. The skyline is dominated by industrial units, including the Honda car manufacturing plant.

This is also a positioning move for 70802 + 70804 + 70805, which will be detrained at Hinksey Yard and used on engineering trains in the Southall and Hayes area over the Easter weekend.

Alan Hazelden

On The Logs .... On 11th July, a Colas Class 70 makes its debut on the Chirk timber traffic.

70802 + 66847 (DIT) (above) sweep through the Lune Valley at Carlingill with 6J37, the 12:02 Carlisle Yard - Chirk loaded timber. The WCML shares the valley with the River Lune, the M6 Motorway and A6 trunk road, with high fells on either side. **Ian Ball**

Rescuing a Colas 60 .... No.70804 (below) comes to the rescue of Colas Class 60 No.60087 'CLIC Sargent' on 23rd July when the 'tug' fails at Hullavington on its maiden run for Colas with 6V62, the 11:13 Tilbury Riverside - Llanwern steel. The ensemble is seen here passing Ram Hill, one mile west of Westerleigh Junction. Oh, the shame! **Edward Gleed**

Background

GBRf became an operator of Class 73 locos in 2004, having bought six redundant Gatwick Express locos, Nos.73203 - 73207 and 73209 .

Nos.73204 - 73206 and 73209 were the first to return to traffic after overhaul by Fragonset at Derby, repainted in the company's blue and orange livery. They were named after female employees and their primary duties were engineering trains working out of Eastleigh and Tonbridge.

Class 73, No.73962 Profile

Built	:	May 1966
Depot	:	Stewarts Lane
Original No.	:	E6032
Re-numbered	:	73125 December 1973
		73204 February 1988
		73902 April 2013
		73962 January 2014
Livery	:	BR Blue
		BR InterCity, Large Logo
		BR InterCity Corporate, with Swallow
		GBRf Blue & Orange
Names	:	'Stewarts Lane 1860 - 1985' September 1985
		'Janice' October 2004
		'Dick Mabbutt' August 2014

Conversion

In 2013, GBRf set out to have five of these locos re-engined as Class 73/9 by Brush Traction Wabtec in Loughborough. The first conversion, No.73962 (formerly No.73204), is fitted with a MTU 1,600hp V8 engine and the frontal appearance is different with the provision of light clusters and the installation of a more central location for the jumper cables. The dual driving positions have been retained, albeit with new driver's controls.

No.73962 (above) is unveiled on 3rd August at the Brush factory at Loughborough, when the loco is named 'Dick Mabbutt', Brush Traction's former group engineer, who died in 2013. The naming ceremony took place during the work's open day, which celebrated 125 years of manufacturing at Brush.   **Edward Gleed**

A further plaque (right) has been placed above the nameplate in recognition of the Class 73 re-engineering programme taking place at Brush.   **Craig Adamson**

"In the TOPS Era

In its final guise prior to conversion, the orange & yellow liveried No.73204 'Janice' (top right) works a Network Rail measurement train (1Q62) on 26th November 2009, which is seen approaching Hoo Jct.. No.73141 tails the four coach formation. **Ian Cuthbertson**

On 7th December 1985, No.73125 'Stewarts Lane 1860 - 1985' (middle) is stabled at Clapham Junction. The loco wears BR InterCity livery with the familiar large white double arrow symbol. **John Chalcraft**

Now sporting INTERCITY livery and swallow branding, No.73204 'Stewarts Lane 1860 - 1985' (below) passes through Horley Station on 12th April 1992 with a Gatwick Express service.

This Class 73 + Mark 2 + Class 489 Luggage Van formation started operating in May 1984, when Mark 2F stock was released from Midland Main Line duties. **Ian Cuthbertson**

A Review of the 2013 RHTT Season

Circuits

There are 19 loco-hauled circuits with motive power diagrammed for:

DRS	: Class 20	Class 37	Class 57	Class 66/4
DBS	: Class 66/0	Class 67		
FHH	: Class 66/5 *			
NR	: Class 97/3			
*	: Class 57/3 (NR) in case of FHH loco failure.			

The Routes

Some of the routes are very circuitous and a RHTT can travel over a section of track several times, spraying each of the running lines in turn, especially where there are instances of four running lines, as on the East Coast and West Coast main lines.

Spraying is also very time consuming, which is why so many of these trains run overnight to minimise disruption to other services. In fact, 3J11 and 3S71 take over 20 hours!

A lack of space prevents full itineraries to be reproduced, but a brief summary of each diagram is given, albeit restricted to the origin and destination, plus locations where a stop for pathing, crewing or a reversal takes place. It should also be noted that different diagrams run on different days of the week, as can be seen by the 3S11 - 3S15 York-based trains

INVERNESS

3S95 : **INVERNESS TC (16:02)** – Moy - Rose Street – Nairn - Forres Loop – Elgin – Keith Loop – Huntly – Kennethmont - Insch - Inverurie - Dyce - Aberdeen - Montrose - Dundee - Perth Down Loop - Dalwhinnie – Inverness TC – Moy – **INVERNESS TC (08:11)**

CARLISLE

3J11 : **CARLISLE (16:13)** - Blea Moor – Blackburn – Preston - Barrow in Furness - Carnforth D & UGL – Windermere – Oxenholme – Carlisle - Carlisle Kingmoor - Preston - Hellifield Goods Loop – Skipton - Hellifield Goods Loop – Whitehaven - **CARLISLE KINGMOOR (13:17)**

3S77 : **CARLISLE KINGMOOR (05:27)** – Wooden Gate Jct. – Little Mill LC – Heaton South Jct. – Newcastle Nunthorpe – Middlesbrough – Middlesbrough Sidings – Low Gates LC – Tursdale Jct. – Hexham – London Road Jct. – Carlisle – **CARLISLE KINGMOOR (16:56)**

CREWE

3S71 : CREWE TMD (18:43) – Crewe – Shrewsbury – Sutton Bridge Jct. – Welshpool – Newtown – Talerddig – Newtown – Welshpool – Sutton Bridge Jct. – Shrewsbury – Craven Arms – Shrewsbury – Bidston – Shrewsbury – Chester – Holywell Jct. – Holyhead – Crewe – **CREWE TMD (15:03)**

Key to abbreviations :

DGL	Down Goods Loop	DPL	Down Passing Loop
FP	Fuelling Point	Jct	Junction
LC	**Level Crossing**	LIP	Loco Inspection Point
TC	Traffic Centre	TMD	Traction Maintenance Depot
TS	Tamper Siding	UGL	Up Goods Loop
UPL	Up Passing Loop	URS	Up Reversing Sidings
WRD	Wagon Repair Depot		

A single DBS Class 66/0 is used on the Inverness-based RHTT. No.66023 (opposite) is seen upon arrival (00:35hrs) at Carnoustie on Saturday, 5th October 2013, with 3S95 ex-Inverness, ready for uncoupling and a run to Arbroath to crossover/reverse.   ---   *Jim Ramsay*

RHTT Loco-Hauled Circuits (Autumn 2013)

Area	Outbase	Train Reporting Codes	Traction
Highlands	Inverness	3S95	DBS 66
Cumbria	Carlisle	3J11	DRS 66s
Tyne / Tees	Carlisle	3S77	DRS 37s
Yorkshire & Humberside	York	3S11, 3S12, 3S13, 3S14, 3S15	DRS 20s
		3S21, 3S22, 3S23, 3S24, 3S25, 3S26	DRS 20s
North Wales	Crewe	3S71	NR 97/3s
East Midlands	Toton	3J87, 3J88	DBS 66s
Midland Main Line	Toton	3J92, 3J93	DBS 67s
WCML (South)	Bescot	3J01	DBS 66s
Lincolnshire	Peterboro'	3J41, 3J42, 3J43, 3J44	DBS 66s
ECML (South)	Peterboro'	3J31, 3J32, 3J33, 3J34, 3J35, 3J36	DBS 66s
East Anglia	Stowmarket	3S60, 3S50	DRS 47s/57s
East Suffolk	Stowmarket	3S01, 3S11	DRS 57s
West Anglia / N. London	Broxbourne	3S81	FHH 66/5s
North Thames / Essex	Broxbourne	3S40	FHH 66/5s
Chilterns & Euston DC Lines	Acton	2S74, 3J04	DBS 66s
GWML	Didcot	3J41, 3J42, 3J43, 3J44	DBS 66s
Welsh Valleys & Severnside	Bristol	3S59	DBS 66s
West Wales	Margam	3S61	DBS 66s
Devon & Cornwall	St. Blazey	3J11, 3J12, 3J13	DBS 66s

37s on RHTT

3S77 : DRS Class 37/4s are the order of the day for the Tyne Valley and Teesside RHTTs. With the famous Transporter Bridge dominating the background, a grimy No.37419 (above) leads 3S77 into Middlesbrough, having run to Nunthorpe to reverse. An equally grimy No.37409 'Lord Hinton' tails.　**Steven Brykajlo**

3S71 : Upon arrival at Craven Arms No.97304, top 'n' tailed with No.97303, waits to reverse after the tail light (the red dot!) had been fitted on the nose of No.97304 (below), which will now be the rear of the train. Craven Arms is the southern limit of operation for train 3S71 on the 'Marches' route.　**Mike Hemming**

3S71 : Network Rail Class 97/3s, operating out of Crewe TMD, have the responsibility of working RHTT diagrams in the Shrewsbury area, North Wales and the Cambrian line to Machynlleth. During an evening lay-over at Shrewsbury on 13th November 2013, Nos.97303 and 97304 (above) are seen in Platform No.5 bay, waiting time and the road to Craven Arms with 3S71.   **Mike Hemming**

3S77 : No.37425 'Sir Robert MacAlpine / Concrete Bob' (below) heads east and away from the camera at Mains Rigg, as it negotiates the sweeping curves in this section of the Tyne Valley, with 3S77; No.37409 tails. This area abounds in Roman history; the railway straddles the site of the old Roman Stanegate Road and to the north of the railway (out of view) is Hadrian's Wall.   **Ian Ball**

YORK (Monday, Wednesday, Friday)

3S11 : YORK WORKS (01:47) – York Yard North - Barnsley - Lockwood - Barnsley - Codnor Park Jct - **CHESTERFIELD (06:15)**

3S12 : CHESTERFIELD (06:21) – Grindleford – Sheffield – Wakefield Kirkgate – Wakefield Westgate – **WRENTHORPE RS (08:40)**

3S13 : WRENTHORPE RS (08:50) – Wakefield Westgate – Thorne Junction – **GRIMSBY TOWN (10:53)**

3S14 : GRIMSBY TOWN (11:12) – Scunthorpe Trent Jct – Hatfield & Stainforth – Sheffield – Church Fenton - **MALTON (16:27)**

3S15 : MALTON (16:32) – York Scarborough Bridge Jct – York Loop (Holgate) – York Yard North RS – **YORK WORKS (17:45)**

(Tuesday and Thursday Only)

3S11 : YORK WORKS (01:47) – Wakefield Westgate - Wakefield Kirkgate - Barnsley - **SHEFFIELD (06:32)**

3S12 : SHEFFIELD (06:58) – Wincobank - Moorthorpe Loop - **SHEFFIELD (09:21)**

3S13 : SHEFFIELD (09:31) – Worksop - **SHEFFIELD (10:34)**

3S14 : SHEFFIELD (11:31) – South Kirby Jct. - Sheffield - Deepcar - Sheffield - **WAKEFIELD KIRK. (17:07)**

3S15 : WAKEFIELD KIRKGATE (17:11) – Milford Signal Box - Hull - Kirk Sandall - Goole - Brough - **YORK WORKS (22:58)**

YORK

3S21 : YORK WORKS (14:53) – York Yard North RS – Leeds Signal L929 – Leeds - Neville Hill West Jct – Barlby Loops – **GILBERDYKE(18:49)**

3S22 : GILBERDYKE (18:59) – Barlby Loops – Leeds Marsh Lane Jct – Leeds – Bradford Interchange – **HALL ROYD JCT. (22:28)**

3S23 : HALL ROYD JCT. (23:10) – Halifax – Huddersfield – Bradford Int. - Shipley – **ILKLEY (02:47)**

3S24 : ILKLEY (02:54) – Apperley Jct – **SKIPTON (04:04)**

3S25 : SKIPTON (04:30) – Leeds – **KNARESBOROUGH (06:31)**

3S26 : KNARESBOROUGH (06:41) – Neville Hill West Jct – **YORK WORKS (09:28)**

3S14 : Coal mining at the Hatfield Mine resumed in April 2007.

The mine forms an impressive backdrop, as Nos.20304 and 20312 (opposite) pass through Hatfield & Stainforth on 7th October 2013 with 3S14, the 11:12 Grimsby Town - Malton RHTT. **Alan Padley**

Meanwhile, on 27th November 2013, the driver of No.20304 (top right) gives a friendly wave as 3S14 comes down the hill at Booths Crossing, near Tilts, on the Stainforth Jct - Skellow Jct 'freight only' line, having just passed Applehurst Jct. **Neil Harvey**

3S12 : Nos.20305 + 20302 (middle) top 'n' tail 3S12, the 06:21 Chesterfield - Wrenthorpe RHTT, as they pass through Grindleford on a damp 11th October 2013. It's dull, the lights are on in the 'bus style' shelter, and there's not a single passenger to be seen. **Mick Tindall**

3S21 : No.20312 and No.20302 (below) top 'n' tail 3S21, the 14:53 York Works - Gilberdyke, as they cross the River Wharfe at Ulleskelf on 7th November 2013. This is a relatively short 'trip', lasting about four hours. **Neil Harvey**

3S14

On 2nd November 2013, Nos.20304 and 20305 (above) pass under the Humber suspension bridge, spraying their way through Hessle station on 2nd November 2013, running as 3S14, the 11:31 Stocksbridge - York, having already visited the Deepcar branch earlier in the day.
Syd Young

It's a new day and a new pair of 'choppers' have been allocated to RHTT 3S14. Nos.20312 and 20302 (below) are seen approaching Selby on their way from Hull to York. The scene is dominated by the famous Selby Swing Bridge which carries the railway line from Leeds to Hull, over the River Ouse.
Alan Padley

Southern Region

Locos **Vice** MPVs

Due to mechanical problems and the side-lining of the southern area Multi Purpose Vehicles (MPVs), some RHTT duties are placed in the hands of GBRf Class 73s and Network Rail Class 57/3 locos.

This proves to be an added bonus and their movements are closely followed by railway enthusiasts living in the South East.

(Left) : On 10th October 2013, Class 73s No.73212 and No.73213 haul RHTT service 6X01 through Paddock Wood, having just been to Ashford and back. The train has to return to Tonbridge Yard as one of the water jet modules has failed.

(Below) : The same pair of 73s are seen again, this time 'spraying' past Frant with 6X01 ex-Tonbridge Yard, aiming to visit as many places as possible during the day! The 'squirty' bits are housed on 'KFAs':

No.99.70.9310.001-1
No.99.70.9310.007-8.

Alan Hazelden (2)

PETERBOROUGH

3J31 : **PETERBOROUGH (01:37)** – Harringay URS – Hitchin – Foxton – **HARRINGAY URS (06:39)**

3J32 : **HARRINGAY URS (05:45)** – Biggleswade – Royston – Foxton – Royston - **HARRINGAY URS (09:14)**

3J33 : **HARRINGAY URS (09:22)** – Hitchin Signal K232 – Hitchin – **PETERBOROUGH LIP (12:26)**

3J34 : **PETERBOROUGH LIP (14:29)** – Connington Loop – Hitchin – Hitchin Up Yard – Royston Loop –
Foxton – Royston - **HARRINGAY URS (18:50)**

3J35 : **HARRINGAY URS (19:01)** – Biggleswade - **HARRINGAY URS (21:06)**

3J36 : **HARRINGAY URS (21:40)** – **PETERBOROUGH LIP (23:27)**

3J41 : **PETERBOROUGH LIP (08:03)** – Lincoln Central - **DONCASTER LIP (10:48)**

3J42 : **DONCASTER (11:30)** – Sleaford – Boston – **PETERBOROUGH EASTFIELD JCT. (15:57)**

3J43 : **PETERBOROUGH EASTFIELD JCT. (16:05)** – Leicester – **PETERBOROUGH LIP (18:36)**

3J44 : **PETERBOROUGH LIP (19:07)** – Grantham – **PETERBOROUGH LIP (00:21)**   (3 return trips)

BESCOT

3JO1 :

BESCOT TMD (10:50)
Rugby
Newcastle Jct (Staffs)
Macclesfield
Rugby
Northampton–
Watford
St. Albans Abbey
London Euston –
BESCOT TMD (06:33)

TOTON

3J87 / 3J88 : **TOTON (02:13)** – Stapleford & Sandiacre – Derby – Ambergate – Matlock – Ambergate –
Derby – Stapleford & Sandiacre – Stenson Jct – Stoke-on-Trent – Crewe – Stoke-on-Trent – Lenton
North Jct – Shirebrook – Kirkby in Ashfield – Nottingham – Newark Castle – Lincoln Central – Holton
Le Moor Signal Box – Lincoln Central – Nottingham – Stapleford & Sandiacre – **TOTON (16:18)**

3J92 : **TOTON (23:18)** – Stapleford & Sandiacretyhj – Bedford North Jct – West Hampstead Thameslink –
Bedford – West Hampstead Thameslink – Nuneaton – Leicester LIP – Bedford North Jct –
WEST HAMPSTEAD NORTH JCT (11:06)

3J93 : **WEST HAMPSTEAD NORTH JCT (11:53)** – Luton - West Hampstead North Jct – Sharnbrook Jct –
Wellingborough DGL – Leicester – Stapleford & Sandiacre – **TOTON TMD (17:23)**

3J42 : On 25th November 2013, No.66040 and No.66044 (above) top 'n' tail 3J42, the 11:30
Doncaster - Peterborough Eastfield Junction RHTT and are seen passing Bessacarr Junction; the
point at which the lines from Black Carr Junction and Decoy South Junction meet.

All the Peterborough RHTTs (3J31 - 3J36 and 3J41 - 3J44) and the two East Midlands diagrams
(3J87 & 3J88) are allocated DBS Class 66/0 traction.   **Alan Padley**

67s on RHTT

3J92 : On 8th October 2013, 3J92 is actually worked by the 'booked' traction of two Class 67 locos! Having been held at Bedford North Junction waiting its path, No.67015 'David J. Lloyd' + No.67020 (above) have just passed Bedford South Junction and are now approaching Elstow.

Here, on 22nd November 2013, No.67008 (below) top 'n' tailed with No.66058, passes Souldrop on the 'Up Fast' line with 3J92. The bi-directional slow line used by the majority of freight services is at a lower level.

3J92 : DBS Class 67 No.67026 'Diamond Jubilee' (above) leads 3J92, the 23:44 Toton - West Hampstead North Jct RHTT past Irthlingborough Road, Wellingborough, on 8th November 2013; Class 66/0 No.66103 on the rear of the formation. This is a popular location with good views to be had in both directions.

3J93 : Away from 'WAG Express' passenger services, ATW No.67003 (below) is seen on 23rd October 2013 crossing onto the 'Down Fast' at Sharnbrook Junction (between Wellingborough and Bedford) top 'n' tailed with Class 66/0 No.66140 on 3J93, the 11:53 West Hampstead North Jct. - Toton TMD.   **Nigel Gibbs (4)**

Freightliner Heavy Haul (FHH) Class 66s have been drafted in for the West Anglia and North London Railhead Treatment Trains. On 29th October 2013, Class 66/5s No.66523 and No.66557 (above) top 'n' tail 3S81, the 07:58 Broxbourne - Broxbourne and are seen crossing the A10 at Foxton on the Great Northern route from London King's Cross to Cambridge.   **Nigel Gibbs**

On 2nd November 2013, one of the FHH-operated Broxbourne-based RHTT sets is worked by Class 66/5 No.66535 and Class 66/6 No.66621 (below), about to enter Crouch Hill station. In theory, this train should have stopped in Upper Holloway 'Up' Goods Loop to allow FHH Class 66/6 No.66605 to pass on an empty cement train, but in the event this didn't happen.   **Nick Slocombe**

3S40 : **BROXBOURNE TS (08:31)** – Hertford East – Broxbourne – Cheshunt – Seven Sisters – Shoeburyness – Leigh on Sea – Gas Factory Loop – West Ham – Pitsea – West Thurrock Jct. - Ockendon – Upminster – Ockendon – Grays – Barking – Seven Sisters Signal L1327 – Cheshunt Jct. Signal L1395 – Broxbourne Down Pass Loop – **BROXBOURNE TS (18:48)**

3S81 : **BROXBOURNE TS (07:58)** – Harlow Town – Whittlesford Down Goods Loop – Cambridge Signal 147 Cambridge – Royston – Royston Loop – Royston – Cambridge – Harlow Town – London Fields – Navarino Road Jct. – Willesden Railnet – Reading Lane Jct. – London Fields - Cheshunt Jct. Signal L1395 – Broxbourne Down Pass Loop – **BROXBOURNE TS (17:05)**

The West Anglia RHTT (3S81) is seen resting in the loop at Royston on 17th October 2013, prior to returning back into Anglia after the 10:15hrs King's Cross - Cambridge express has passed. The train locos are No.57305 and No.57301 (above), which are standing in due to the non-availability of the 'booked' FHH 66s. Signal K980 is 'off' for the 09:55 Cambridge - King's Cross stopper. **Nigel Gibbs**

(Overleaf) :

(Page 190) : DRS Class 37/4s, No.37409 'Lord Hinton' and No.37425 'Sir Robert MacAlpine / Concrete Bob' (top) top n' tail 3S77, Carlisle - Carlisle RHTT on 9th November 2013. The train is passing Great Corby, a village above the eastern bank of a wooded gorge on the River Eden. Directly across the river from Great Corby is the village of Wetheral; the two villages linked by a railway viaduct. **Steven Brykajlo**

Network Rail Class 57/3s make a welcome appearance on southern metals, vice MPVs. No.57396 (bottom) passes Stone Crossing station on 13th November 2013 working 6X01, the 10:01 Tonbridge West Yard - Tonbridge West Yard RHTT. Are the wind turbines a blot on the landscape? **Ian Cuthbertson**

(Page 191) : Class 73s are also out and about in Kent. No.73141 and No.73119 (top) work the 'South Eastern area' Rail Head Treatment Train on 3rd November 2013 and pass Folkestone Warren with 6X01, consisting of 'KFA' flats No.99.70.9310.006-0 and No.99.70.9310.005-2. **Richard A. Jones**

Perfect timing, two trains caught in a patch of sunlight on 24th October 2013. 'Sheds' No.66139 and No.66134 (bottom) wait to cross over onto the Uttoxeter lines at North Staffs Junction with 3J88, the 02:13 Toton - Toton RHTT, as Arriva Trains Class 175 No.170519 hurries past in the opposite direction with a service bound for Nottingham. **Syd Young**

STOWMARKET

3S60 : **STOWMARKET DGL (04:54)** – Trowse Swing Bridge – Trowse Yard – Wymondham - Signal W32 - Trowse Yard – Claydon – Witham – Shenfield – Mountnessing Jct. – Southend Victoria – Shenfield - Witham – Clacton on Sea – Colchester - Ipswich – Claydon – **STOWMARKET DGL (17:54)**

3S50 : **STOWMARKET DGL (18:14)** – Harwich – Norwich – Ely – Norwich – **STOWMARKET DGL (01:24)**

3S11 : **STOWMARKET DGL (18:14)** – Marks Tey UPL - Shenfield – Southend Victoria – Romford – Upminster - Stratford - Shenfield - Stratford - Braintree - Witham - **STOWMARKET DGL (05:43)**

3S01 : **STOWMARKET DGL (09:20)** – Cromer – Norwich – Ipswich - Lowestoft - Norwich - Acle - Brundall - Diss - **STOWMARKET DGL (18:17)**

57002 + 57003

DRS Class 57s No.57002 + No.57003 (top) are seen working 3S60, 04:54 Stowmarket D.G.L. - Stowmarket D.G.L. RHTT circuit on 30th October 2013, 'under the wires', heading along Belstead Bank, just south of Ipswich, on the Great Eastern Main Line.

In this view, on the same day, No.57002 (above) brings up the rear of 3S60, as spraying takes place through Manningtree station; No.57003 is the leading loco. **Ian Cuthbertson (2)**

'Preparing For Action'

After a spell of maintenance, one of the Stowmarket RHTT set of wagons returns for spraying duties and DRS Class 57s No.57004 and No.57009 (above) pass Bessacarr Junction, Doncaster, on 25th November 2013, running on this occasion as 6Z65, York Works - Stowmarket. **Alan Padley**

Meanwhile, on 23rd September 2013, DRS Class 57/0 No. 57004 (below) is seen on the 'joint line' at Gosberton, between Sleaford and Spalding, with the 2013 RHTT 'leaf-busting' season vehicles for Anglia. The train is 6Z32, the 09:40 York Works - Stowmarket, which has just passed East Midlands 'Sprinter' No.153326 on the 'down' line working 2T46, the 12:41 Peterborough - Lincoln Central. **Nigel Gibbs**

ACTON

2S74 : **ACTON TC (21:34)** - London Euston - Watford Jct. - **LONDON EUSTON (00:05)**

3J04 : **LONDON EUSTON (00:27)** - Acton Main Line - Aynho Signal Bs5002 - Princes Risborough - Aylesbury - Aylesbury Parkway - Amersham - Aylesbury - London Marylebone - Aylesbury - Aylesbury Sidings 1 to 7 - Aylesbury - London Marylebone - South Ruislip - **ACTON TC (11:48)**

DIDCOT

3J41 : **DIDCOT FP (14:51)** - Didcot Parkway - Ufton Loop - Westbury - Theale Loop - **DIDCOT FP (19:21)**

3J42 : **DIDCOT FP (20:53)** - Southall - Basingstoke - **DIDCOT TC (00:02)**

3J43 : **DIDCOT TC (03;58)** - Didcot East Jct. - Swindon - **DIDCOT PARKWAY (05:08)**

3J44 : **DIDCOT PARKWAY (05:28)** - Reading - West Ealing Loop - Kennet Bridge Loop - Didcot Parkway - **DIDCOT FP (09:01)**

BRISTOL BARTON HILL

3S59 : **BRISTOL BARTON HILL WRD (19:21)** - Bristol Temple Meads - Chippenham - Bath Goods Loop - Bristol Temple Meads - Westbury - Clifton Down - Avonmouth - St. Andrews Jct. - Cardiff Central - Radyr – Cardiff Central - Abercynon - Merthyr Tydfil - Abercynon - Pontypridd - Mountain Ash - Cardiff Central - Ebbw Vale Parkway - Newport - Gloucester - Newport - Gloucester - Haresfield - Loop - Bristol Parkway - Avonmouth - Clifton Down - Bristol Temple Meads - Weston Super Mare - Bristol Temple Meads - **BRISTOL BARTON HILL WRD (15:26)**

MARGAM

3S61 : **MARGAM TC (18:57)** - Cardiff Central - Coryton - Heath Jct. - Bargoed - Tir-phil - Bargoed - Cardiff Central - Leckwith North Jct. - Tondu - Maesteg - Tondu - Bridgend - Margam TC - Whitland - Tenby - Pembroke Dock - Tenby - Whitland - Clarbeston Road - Fishguard Harbour - Clarbeston Rd Haverfordwest - Milford Haven - Clarbeston Road - Margam TC - Pencoed Up Passenger Loop - Miskin - Cardiff Central - Bargoed - Cardiff Central - **MARGAM TC (15:32)**

ST BLAZEY

3J11 : **ST. BLAZEY LIP (20:18)** - St. Blazey Signal box - Par - Penzance - **PAR (00:55)**

3J12 : **PAR (01:21)** - Newton Abbot - Paignton - Exeter St Davids - Topsham - Exmouth - Topsham - Exeter St Davids - Crediton - Exeter St Davids - Taunton – **WESTBURY (08:40)**

3J13 : **WESTBURY (08:45) -** Salisbury - Westbury Down TC - Exeter St Davids - Plymouth - Par - St. Blazey Signal Box - **ST BLAZEY LIP (15:42)**

3J04 : On 3rd November 2013, RHTT 3J04, the 08:47 London Euston - Amersham is seen in the Chilterns, top 'n' tailed by Nos.66019 and 66017 (top left). The 'sheds' are returning from Bicester North and are, approaching Haddenham & Thame Parkway. **Geoff Plumb**

3J13 : On 15th October 2013, Nos.66074 + 66187 (bottom left) double head a very late running 3J13, 8:45 Westbury - St. Blazey LIP, passing Shaldon road bridge, Teignmouth.
Robert Sherwood

3S59 : On 17th October 2013, the Barton Hill RHTT (top right) passes through Yatton and meets Class 150 No.150106 departing on 2Y16, 12:12 Bristol Parkway - Weston-super-Mare. The RHTT consist is No.66098 + 'KFAs' 642017 & 642002 + No.66126. **Chris Perkins**

3S61: Working the Rhymney branch on 23rd October 2013, Nos.66161 and 66250 (bottom right) pass through Hengoed, with 3S61, the 18:57 Margam - Margam. **Peter Slater**

Background History

Thirty years ago in 1984, the Government and British Rail gave formal notice of its intention to close the Settle & Carlisle railway line. There was outrage; local authorities and rail enthusiasts joined forces to save the line, advocating the need of a diversionary route for the West Coast Main Line, and that British Rail failed to promote through traffic via the 'S & C' from the Midlands and Yorkshire to Scotland.

The campaign uncovered evidence that British Rail had mounted a 'dirty tricks' campaign, by exaggerating the cost of repairs (£6 million for Ribblehead Viaduct alone) and diverting traffic away from the line to justify its closure plans, a process referred to as ***"closure by stealth"***.

However, when closure notices were posted on the remaining stations, the reverse effect was actually achieved with increased passenger numbers - rising from 93,000 in 1983 to 450,000 by 1989. In conjunction with local authorities, eight of the closed stations were reopened. Ironically, as BR did not wish to invest in new trains for the line, a combination of first-generation DMUs (used on local stopping trains) and Class 31s / Class 47s (hauling the 'faster' expresses), generated added interest and revenue, especially amongst rail enthusiasts.

Saved for the Nation

Twenty Five years ago, May 1989, the Right Honourable Michael Portillo, Minister of Transport, announced that closure was being declined as a result of the great public interest shown in the line and that the actual cost of repairing Ribblehead viaduct would be considerably less than originally anticipated. It was also hoped the great public interest displayed in saving the line could be turned into a means of creating greater posterity for the Settle & Carlisle.

Commemoration

"Line By Line" : Following in the footsteps of the successful *'Line By Line'* series, this special edition celebrates *25 years* since this famous railway line was saved from closure.

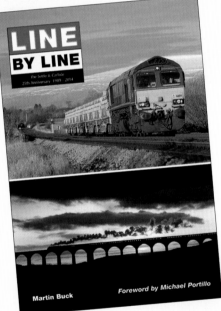

The journey begins at Hellifield, travelling north over the *'Long Drag'* to the Border City of Carlisle using images to illustrate the locos, rolling stock and services at work on the 'S & C' since 1989.

There is expansive text and captions, gradient profiles, route diagrams showing the running lines, stations, signalling, tunnels & viaducts, plus personal anecdotes of my own 'S & C' memories.

This Book can be obtained from :

www.freightmasterpublishing.co.uk

Retail price : £18.95.

Special Train : The focus of celebrations is a special train ("S & C Anniversary Express") on Friday 11 April, supplied and crewed by Direct Rail Services (DRS), comprising three DRS Class 37 locos and a set of recently refurbished Mark 2 vehicles.

This train runs between Leeds to Carlisle, travelling over the 'S & C' in both directions.

A small portfolio of images is included to illustrate the run.

1Z37 : On the outward journey, DRS Class 37s No.37259 + 37425 'Sir Robert MacAlpine/Concrete Bob' (above) accelerate away from the north portal of Blea Moor Tunnel on 11th April with 1Z37, the 09:30 Leeds - Carlisle 'S & C Anniversary Express'; No.37409 is on the rear of the train, out of shot. The stock for the charter had arrived at Leeds via Hexham, Durham and York, formed of 10 Mark 2 vehicles. **Jamie Squibbs**

1Z38 : (Overleaf) : Nos.37259 + 37425 'Sir Robert MacAlpine/Concrete Bob' storm out of Culgaith Tunnel and past the 284 miles and 60 chains milepost on the approach to Culgaith crossing with the return 1Z38, the 14:32 Carlisle - Leeds. **Keith McGovern**

Meanwhile, further south, No.37409 'Lord Hinton' (below) brings up the rear of 1Z38 as Nos.37259 + 37425 head away from the camera at Foredale, Helwith Bridge. From here the railway shares the valley with the B6479 and the River Ribble, before narrowing to go through a gorge at Stainforth. **Neil Harvey**

Background

The Grand Depart

For only the second time in this great race's history, the *'Tour De France'* starts off in the United Kingdom, in Leeds, with three stages before moving across the Channel to France. The only other time being in 2007, when the Race started in London.

Yorkshire hosts two stages:

Stage 1 : Leeds to Harrogate   190km   Saturday, 5th July
Stage 2 : York to Sheffield   201km   Sunday, 6th July

What sounded like a strange idea when a Yorkshire start was first mooted two years ago, turns out to be the biggest, most spectacular *Grand Depart* in the Tour's history, with an estimated four million people over two days lining the route in Yorkshire.

Special Trains Laid On

With so many people visiting Yorkshire, the Transport Passenger Executive lay on special trains (mostly loco-hauled!) to bring people to the event; in fact, almost a quarter of a million people pass through Leeds station on Saturday, 5th July!

"Loco-hauled trains over the Trans-Pennine routes for the first time in over 20 years"

BRADFORD INTERCHANGE

1Z17 : Two loco-hauled trains present at one time must, nowadays, be a rare event at Bradford Interchange, but not on 6th July when extra trains operated in conjunction with the Tour de France cycle race. DRS Class 47 No.47810 'Peter Bath MBE 1927-2006' (above) heads the delayed 1Z17, 13:05hrs shuttle service to Blackburn, via Copy Pit, while DBS Class 67 No.67027 sits in the adjacent platform at the rear of 5L03 ECS. Given that the other platforms are occupied by a Class 150 and Class 158 on service trains, a stabled Grand Central Class 180, Bradford Interchange is truly full-up!   **John Whitehouse**

(Previous Page)

LYDGATE VIADUCT

1Z16 : On 6th July, DRS Class 57/3 No.57308 'County Of Staffordshire' crosses Lydgate Viaduct, between Cornholme and Todmorden, with 1Z16, the 11:43 Blackburn - Bradford Interchange. **Neil Harvey**

Yorkshire Loco-Hauled Diagrams

SET 1 :

Northern Rail - operated by Direct Rail Services / TnT 47/57 with Riviera stock / DRS Stock

Saturday

1Z20, 10:35 Leeds - Harrogate	1Z21, 11:20 Harrogate - Leeds
1Z22, 12:01 Leeds - Harrogate	1Z23, 12:49 Harrogate - Leeds
1Z24, 13:30 Leeds - Harrogate	1Z25, 14:18 Harrogate - Leeds
1Z26, 15:05 Leeds - Harrogate	1Z27, 15:50 Harrogate - Leeds
1Z28, 16:34 Leeds - Harrogate	1Z29, 17:18 Harrogate - Leeds
1Z30, 18:04 Leeds - Harrogate	1Z31, 18:54 Harrogate - Leeds
1Z32, 19:37 Leeds - Harrogate	1Z33, 20:19 Harrogate - Leeds
1Z34, 21:30 Leeds - Harrogate	1Z35, 22:17 Harrogate - Leeds
1Z36, 23:02 Leeds - Harrogate	1Z37, 23:44 Harrogate - Leeds

Sunday

1Z15, 10:21 Bradford Interchange - Blackburn	1Z16, 11:43 Blackburn - Bradford Interchange
1Z17, 13:05 Bradford Interchange - Blackburn	1Z18, 14:25 Blackburn - Bradford Interchange
1Z19, 15:40 Bradford Interchange - Blackburn	1Z20, 17:17 Blackburn - Bradford Interchange
1Z21, 18:57 Bradford Interchange - Blackburn	1Z22, 20:21 Blackburn - Bradford Interchange

SET 2 :

Northern Rail - operated by DB Schenker / TnT 67s with Virgin Trains "Pretendolino" WB64 Mark 3 set

Saturday

1H01, 11:15 Leeds - Harrogate	1H02, 11:54 Harrogate - Leeds
1H03, 13:15 Leeds - Harrogate	1H04, 13:54 Harrogate - Leeds
1H05, 14:36 Leeds - Harrogate	1H06, 15:19 Harrogate - Leeds
1H09, 19:15 Leeds - Harrogate	1H10, 19:54 Harrogate - Leeds
1H11, 20:39 Leeds - York	1H12, 22:30 York - Leeds

Sunday

1Z10, 07:00 Leeds - Harrogate	1Z11, 07:35 Harrogate - Leeds
1L01, 08:29 Leeds - Hebden Bridge	1L03, 10:36 Leeds - Hebden Bridge
1L02, 14:19 Hebden Bridge - Leeds	1L04, 17:18 Hebden Bridge - Leeds

SET 3 :

Trans Pennine Express - operated by Direct Rail Services / TnT 47s with DRS stock

Saturday	Sunday
1Z80, 06:22 Liverpool Lime St. - Scarborough	1Z80, 06:00 Liverpool Lime St. - York
1Z85, 09:50 Scarborough - Liverpool Lime St.	1Z82, 12:00 York - Manchester Piccadilly
1Z87, 13:22 Liverpool Lime St. - Scarborough	1Z84, 14:00 Manchester Piccadilly - Doncaster
1Z82, 16:50 Scarborough - Liverpool Lime St.et	1Z86, 17:50 Doncaster - Liverpool Lime St.

Excludes ECS Movements

COPY PIT : **(1Z37)** : DRS Class 47/8 No.47810 'Peter Bath MBE 1927-2008' (above), sporting the new Compass livery, approaches Copy Pit Summit on 6th July with a late-running 1Z17, the 13:05 Bradford Interchange - Blackburn. The driver is anxiously looking back at his loco and, as it transpires, No.'810 is declared a failure at Blackburn and DRS Class 20s No.20308 + No.20309 take over!   **Neil Harvey (2)**

DRYCLOUGH JUNCTION : **(1L01)** : On 6th July, DBS corporate liveried Class 67 No.67027 (below) pulls away from Dryclough Junction, Halifax, with 1L01, the 08:29 Leeds - Hebden Bridge. It is heading for Milner Royd Junction, where it will join the Calder Valley main line. The other lines head east to Greetland Junction.

HALIFAX VIADUCT : (1L04) : On 6th July, the late running 17:18hrs Hebden Bridge - Leeds slips over Halifax Viaduct. DBS Class 67 No.67027 and DVT No 82146 (above) are positioned at the rear of the train, which is being hauled by DBS Class 67 No.67006 'Queens Messenger' (out of picture).   **John Whitehouse**

ROTHERHAM MASBOROUGH : (1Z84) : Also on 6th July, No.47853 'Rail Express' (below) heads 1Z84, the 14:00 Manchester Piccadilly - Doncaster through the former platforms at Rotherham Masborough station; No.47813 is on the rear of the six coach formation. The 'Old Road' on the left bypasses Sheffield Midland station and links up with the Sheffield - Derby main line at Tapton Junction, Chesterfield.   **Alan Padley**

MILL LANE JUNCTION
(1Z16)

It is reminiscent of when His Holiness Pope Paul II visited the UK in 1982, additional loco-hauled services laid on to cater for the anticipated increase in the number of people wishing to attend a big event. This time it's for the *'Tour De France'* visiting Yorkshire and a number of loco-hauled additional workings are laid on. One such working on Sunday, 6th July, is a shuttle service between Blackburn and Bradford Interchange running via Copy Pit and Hebden Bridge. The late morning working from Blackburn (1Z16) is seen carefully descending the 1 in 50 approach to Bradford Interchange, passing Mill Lane signal box, with DRS Class 57 No.57308 'County of Staffordshire' (below) leading and DRS Class 47 No.47810 at the rear. The Class 47 is later substituted by a pair of DRS Class 20s and note the embellishments to the Class 57, including the buffers being decorated with cycle spokes together with an appropriate headboard! **John Whitehouse**

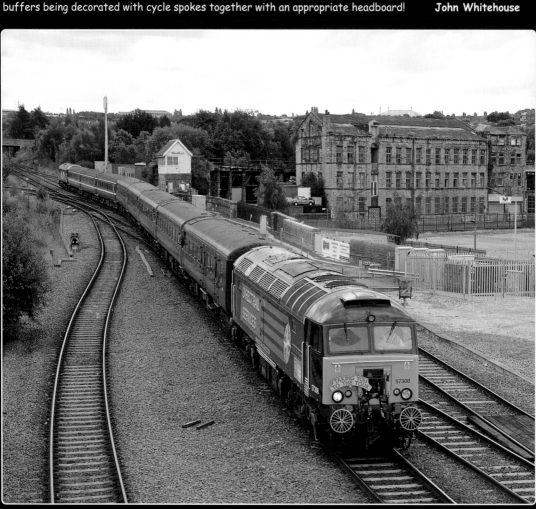

SWINTON (Thryburgh Branch)
(1Z86)

DRS Class 47/8 No.47813 'Solent' (top right), top 'n' tailed with No.47853 'Rail Express', heads past Swinton Bridge (between Mexborough Junction and Aldwarke Junction) on the 'freight-only' line, which avoids Swinton station, with 1Z86, 17:50 Doncaster - Liverpool Lime Street. This particular diagram is routed via Sheffield Midland and the Hope Valley. **Alan Padley**

PADDOCK CUTTING
(1Z85)

DRS Class 47/8 No.47841 (bottom right) passes through Paddock Cutting, Huddersfield, on 5th July at the head of 1Z85, the 09:50 Scarborough - Liverpool Lime Street. Note the painted yellow buffers on the leading loco; No.47853 is on the rear. **Neil Harvey**

ECS Movements

"Think Once, Think Twice, Think Bike"

5Z31 : With many roads closed due to the Tour De France in Yorkshire, Network Rail lay on a standby train to move bikes in case of breakdown. The train is formed of Northern Belle baggage car No.92904, straddled by a DRS class 20 on either end. No.20303 and No.20305 'Gresty Bridge' (above) are seen with the baggage car at Church Fenton on 1st July, running as 5Z31, 14:40 Derby RTC - York.

5L01 : After 1L01 arrives at Hebden Bridge, it's a swift turnaround and the stock returns to Leeds for another 'Tour De France' extra. Here, royal 'skip' No.67006 'Royal Sovereign' (opposite) runs past the cobbles in the outskirts of Halifax near Dryclough Junction with 5L01, the 09:15 Hebden Bridge - Leeds, formed of a section of the Virgin Trains 'Pretendolino' WB64 Mark 3 set.   **Neil Harvey (2)**

ECS Movements

Saturday

SET 1 :

5Z19, 06:12 Crewe H.S. - Leeds

SET 2 :

5Z70, 04:30 Wembley E.F.O.C. - Leeds
5H06, 15:59 Leeds - Neville Hill
5H09, 18:52 Neville Hill - Leeds

SET 3 :

5Z80, 04:51 Crewe H.S. - Liverpool Lime Street
5Zxx, xx:xx Liverpool Lime Street to Edge Hill

Sunday

5Z40, 00:20 Leeds - Bradford Interchange
5Zxx, xx:xx Bradford Interchange - Crewe H.S

5L01, 09:15 Hebden Bridge - Leeds
5L03, 11:34 Hebden Bridge - Bradford Interchange
5L02, 13:35 Bradford Interchange - Hebden Bridge
5L04, 16:16 Leeds to Hebden Bridge
5Zxx, xx:xx Leeds - Wembley E.F.O.C.

5Z80, 05:35 Edge Hill - Liverpool Lime Street
5Z81, 08:35 York - York Holgate Siding
5Z82, 11:41 York Holgate Siding - York
5Z84, 15:53 Doncaster - Doncaster C.H.S.
5Z86, 17:15 Doncaster C.H.S. - Doncaster
5Z87, 21:10 Liverpool Lime Street - Crewe H.S.

LAST SIZEWELL FLASKS

A pair of DRS Class 37s, No.37610 'T.S. (Ted) Cassady 14.5.61 - 6.4.08' + No.37218 (above), heads along the Great Eastern Main Line at Ingatestone on Wednesday, 6th August, with 6M69, the 15:42 Sizewell - Crewe; the final flask train following the removal of all spent fuel rods from Sizewell 'A' power station. Due to obvious secrecy, this flask service was often referred to as the Sizewell 'Coal'.

The power station was shut down on 31st December 2006 and the Nuclear Decommissioning Authority (NDA) budgeted for the decommissioning of Sizewell 'A' at a cost of £1.2 billion.

Images like this on the East Suffolk line will now be consigned to history. On 16th April, DRS Class 20/3s No.20304 + No.20302 (below) pass alongside the boat yards on the River Deben and arrive at Woodbridge in Suffolk with 6L70, the 01:27 Crewe - Sizewell empty flasks.   **Stuart Chapman (2)**

Author's Gallery

'THE WIDER PICTURE'

(Above) : Record breaker? On 8th September, GBRf Class 66/7 No.66753 heads a convoy of nine new GBRf locos - Nos.66757,66758,66765,66759,66760,66762,66761,66764 and 66763, which are passing East Usk Junction, Newport, running as 0X66, Newport Docks - Doncaster Roberts Road.

On 10th July, five locos (Nos.66752/53/54/55 and 56) arrived as the first batch of 21 new Class 66 locos from the USA, which will take the GBRf Class 66 fleet to 71. These are being secured ahead of the change in EU emissions legislation which, from January 2015, sees new regulations coming into force that could impact the ability to obtain compliant and affordable locos. **Chris Davies**

(Top right) : Running as a special 6R71, Immingham - Drax, FHH Class 70.No.70001 is laid on for the official opening of the Joan Croft flyover on 26th June, attended by Transport Minister, Patrick McLoughlin.

It was in October 2012 when the Secretary of State for Transport approved Network Rail's application for a railway flyover at Shaftholme, to the north of Doncaster. The scheme, known as the 'North Doncaster Chord', takes slow moving freight trains travelling from the Humber ports up and over the ECML rather than across and along it. Diverting freight traffic frees up capacity for much needed passenger services and enables additional freight to be transported by rail, rather than road.

(Middle) : After waiting for a couple of hours for the 86's, guess what comes along at exactly the wrong time! However, this turns out to be a rewarding composition; a Virgin Trains Pendolino overtaking a pair of Class 86/6s, No.86622 + No.86610 which, in turn, are overtaking a Class 170 unit No.170632 coming off the Cannock and Rugeley line. The respective services are:

> 1F18, 14:07 London Euston - Liverpool Lime Street
>
> 4M54, 10:10 Tilbury - Crewe Basford Hall
>
> 2K66, 14:12 Birmingham New Street - Rugeley Trent Valley

(Bottom Right) : Having been as far as High Marnham, DRS Class 37s No.37612 and No.37667 top 'n' tail are seen returning with 1Q13 ex-Doncaster on 28th February passing the reception sidings at Thoresby Colliery Junction; the limit of freight services (ie. coal) on this line.

The colliery is reached via the 'Robin Hood' line, which links Nottingham - Kirkby in Ashfield - Mansfield - Shirebrook - Worksop, with the branch leaving this line by means of either Shirebrook Junction or Shirebrook East Junction, to the south and north of Shirebrook, respectively. **Alan Padley (3)**

(Previous Page) : Viewed through the station waiting room window, Colas Class 66/8 No.66850 waits in the sidings at Ribblehead Virtual Quarry with a trainload of timber bound for Chirk. **Syd Young**

'RAISING STEAM'

In its purest form, there can be little to compare with a steam engine working at full throttle on a steep gradient, like this image taken from the archives. LMS Stanier Class 5MT 4-6-0 No.45407 (above) is approaching the summit of the 1 in 90 climb from Chapel-en-le-Frith to Dove Holes, before dropping down into Buxton on 30th November 2008 with 1Z31, the 10:56 Manchester Victoria - Buxton charter. **Alan Padley**

Working at full capacity, tons of evaporated water rise into the atmosphere from all six cooling towers Ferrybridge is doing its bit for the National Grid as another 'grid', DCR No.56312 'Jeremiah Dixon' (top left) passes by on 9th November 2013 with 6Z22, the 06:34 Thoresby - York Holgate empty 'JRA' box wagons The train is crossing the River Aire at Brotherton on the 'Down Pontefract' main line. **Alan Padley**

Timber trains for Kronospan have to pass the plant and reverse into the sidings. At that point, the loco is normally in Chirk station where it can be photographed, but you have to be prepared as it may be stationary for less than 60 seconds; on 10th July, it's three minutes. No.56105 (bottom left) pauses as, through a gap in the trees, steam can be seen rising from the plant into the night sky - delightful! **Colin Partinator**

"Blue and Yellow Don't Make Green" - A Different Perspective

It's actually mixing yellow and cyan that makes green colours, but I digress .... here we have two offerings away from the normal three quarter shot view to provide a different type of composition, where the train is not necessarily the main focus of attention!

On 17th March, DBS liveried Class 66/0 No.66101 (above) waits to depart Didcot Parkway with 4O40, the 08:21 Oxford Morris Cowley - Southampton Eastern Docks car train. The daffodils are bursting into bloom and the platform is graced with the presence of an ex-GWR bench.

Meanwhile, on the same day, DBS Class 66/0 No.66099 (below) passes the daffodils at Basingstoke station with 4V38, the 13:50 Eastleigh Yard - Didcot Yard 'wagonload' service. The distinctive 'WIA', 5-unit, articulated, enclosed car carriers add a splash of blue to the proceedings.   **Mark Pike (2)**

'Off the Peg'

Semaphore signals add a certain *'je ne sais quoi'* and provide an added dimension, provenance and historical perspective to railway photography. There are excellent examples to be found all around the network, but modernisation is quickly catching up in some areas and MAS is replacing some old 'pegs'!

"Do I feel lucky?" A pheasant contemplates crossing the tracks in the face of an approaching 2,000 tonne coal train at Gilberdyke on 2nd April; Class 66/5 No.66519 (above) is on 6M49, the 08.00 Hull Kingston Terminal - Rugeley power station coal. Note the 'switchback' and wonderful old semaphores.   **David Hayes**

On the second day of Spring, 22nd March, amidst some fine examples of ex-GWR lower quadrant semaphore signals, FHH Class 70 No.70014 (below) is seen entering Shrewsbury station off the Chester line with 6Y02, Wrexham - Crewe Basford Hall engineers service (running via Wellington and Stafford).   **Mike Hemming**

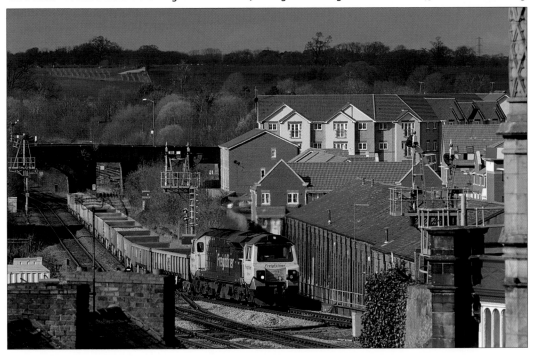

'ARCHITECTURALLY SPEAKING'

A little thought and imagination can result in some interesting compositions ......

River Usk bridge, Newport : *Viewed from the west bank, DVT No.82308 + No.67002 (above) cross the River Usk as they approach Newport on 8th September with 1V91, the 05:30 Holyhead - Cardiff Central. Of particular note is the decorative ironmongery.* **Mark Pike**

Hatfield & Stainforth station : *On 5th March, DBS Class 66/0 No.66130 (below) heads away from the camera after passing through the station with 6E32, the 08:55 Preston Docks - Lindsey empty bitumen tanks. One's eye is drawn to the mass of steelwork, which acts as a footbridge and, just like the one at Barnetby, is an eyesore which is visible from space! It's simply health & safety gone mad, there must be easier and more practical ways to enable passengers to cross from one platform to another.* **Alan Padley**

'TAKING ON THE BANKS'

The challenge of Beattock : *Beattock is legendary, for the simple reason that it provides northbound trains travelling on the West Coast Main Line to Glasgow with a stiff climb. The summit is 50 miles north of Carlisle, but the sting is that the last 15 of those miles are against the grade, the last 10 particularly fearsome. The challenge starts just after Wamphray, when the gradient becomes a gentle climb no greater than 1 in 202 through to the site of Beattock station, after which it stiffens to 1 in 88 initially, then to an average of around 1 in 75 to the summit, peaking at 1 in 69 at Greskine.*

On 29th April, 'Royal Scot' No.46115 'Scots Guardsman' (above) powers 1Z60. the 09:45 Grange over Sands - Edinburgh Waverley leg of the 'Great Britain VII' through Harthope, on the last stage of the climb to Beattock Summit. This 'side-on' view is a pleasant alternative to a three quarter shot view. **John Whitehouse**

(Overleaf)

Shap Attack : *Unlike Beattock, the ascent to Shap Summit is gruelling in both directions. Northbound, after a brief spell of level running past Low Gill, the WCML climbs for two miles at 1 in 146 through Tebay, followed by four miles of climb at 1 in 75, passing Scout Green before reaching Shap Summit.*

Southbound, after leaving Penrith, the line faces eight miles at a steady gradient of 1 in 125 to Shap before briefly levelling out, then a final stretch of 1 in 106 and 1 in 130 to the summit.

(Page 218) : *'Classic Shap'. This is reminiscent of a time when the 'Duchesses' were prime motive power on the crack Anglo-Scottish expresses, like 'The Caledonian'. On Friday, 12th September, LMS Stanier 4-6-2 Pacific No.46233 'Duchess of Sutherland' leans into the curve at Greenholme heading 1Z82, the 13:42 Crewe - Polmont SRPS excursion. No.46233 symbolises the power of the Stanier design in the final BR configuration of the post-war streamlined engines. The author's personal view is that the visual appearance of a 'Duchess' was enhanced by the presence of a double chimney and smoke deflectors.* **John Whitehouse**

(Page 219) : *Thinking ahead, this image leads nicely into the next category - 'Whilst I'm waiting' - and one which breaks the mold, the inclusion of an EMU ('Pendolino') in Loco Review for the first time in 10 years!*

Whilst passing the time in the car at Greenholme, the photographer could not resist trying to catch an image like this; really black clouds in the background and a train bathed in sunshine in the foreground. What a cracking result, on 12th May, at the same location as the previous image, an unidentified Class 390 'Pendolino

'WHILST I'M WAITING'

Costa Colas' : After a hard day, what better way to pass the time, enjoying a good cup of coffee and watching the trains go by - sheer bliss!

For the record, the coffee is a Cappuccino and the train is 6J37, the 12:58 Carlisle Yard - Chirk loaded timber, which is seen crossing Church Street, hauled by an unidentified Colas Class 56 (above); no prizes for guessing where it is!

If this type of image whets your appetite, then there's two more opposite.

'A Touch of Pink' : "Chamerion Angustifolium" - otherwise known as Rosebay Willowherb in the UK and Fireweed in North America - brings a welcome touch of colour to a railway embankment in Northwich. Such delightful lighting is too good an opportunity to misss and the cameraman even bagged his planned shot of FHH Class 66/6 No.66606 working 6M58, the 04:46 Westbury Lafarge - Tunstead cement empties!

'Love is in the Air' : In the outskirts of Buxton, one fine day in June, a heavy train of limestone (6H22, Tunstead - Hindlow) strains on the climb to Hindlow and passes an old and derelict telegraph pole. A pair of Collar Doves sit cosily side by side, completely unphased by what's going on around them, perhaps they have other things on their mind!   **David Hayes (3)**

100 Years On - "Lest We Forget"

On 6th June, Class 66/0 No.66221 (above) stands at Bletchley with 6H10, the 10:07 (TFO) Bletchley - Peak Forest empty stone hoppers; two poppies act as a reminder that 2014 is the 100th anniversary of the outbreak of World War 1, Monday, 4th August 1914.

The poppy is synonymous with acts of remembrance leading up to Armistice Day, 11th November, in honour of the fallen in the Great War, World War II and other conflicts around the world.

"Lest we forget" is an extract from Rudyard Kipling's 1897 poem 'Recessional' and is also the slogan for the POW/MIA (Prisoners of War / Missing In Action) campaign, reminding us to remember, not only the sacrifices of the military as a whole but, the ULTIMATE sacrifice made by those who have, in the course of action become lost or captured by the enemy.

Craig Adamson

Photographers

Name & Website Address

Craig Adamson (flickr.com/photos/37260)	**John Baker**
Ian Ball (northeastheavy60.uk)	**Alastair Blackwood** (flickr.com/photos/30868113)
Steven Brykajlo (steve-b24.smugmug.com)	**John Chalcraft** (railphotoprints.zenfolio.com)
Stuart Chapman	**Martin Cook** (martin-cook.smugmug.com)
Ian Cuthbertson (flickr.com/photos/locohunter)	**Michael Davies** (flickr.com/photos/32755955@N05)
Chris Davies (flickr.com/photos/99220921@N03)	**Neil Downing** (flickr.com/photos/neildowning)
Nigel Gibbs (flickr.com/photos/gibbo53)	**Edward Gleed**
Neil Harvey (flickr.com/neil_harvey_railway_photos)	**David Hayes** (flickr.com/photos/davidhayes)
Alan Hazelden (alanhazelden.smugmug.com)	**Mike Hemming** (flickr.com/photos/d1021)
Derek Holmes	**Guy Houston** (flickr.com/photos/37001)
Simon Howard (sisuktrainpix.smugmug.com)	**Richard A. Jones** (flickr.com/photos/richardajones)
Fred Kerr	**Steven King** (stevekingrailphotos.weebly.com)
Martin Loader (hondawanderer.com)	**Keith McGovern** (flickr.com/photos/16359167@N07)
Alan Padley (flickr.com/photos/alanpadley)	**Philip Parker** (flickr.com/photos/34005859@N03)
Colin Partington (flickr.com/photos/yogzfots)	**Chris Perkins** (transportmedia.smugmug.com)
Mark Pike (mvp-photography.co.uk)	**Geoff Plumb** (plumbloco.smugmug.com)
Jim Ramsay (tayrail.smugmug.com)	**Robert Sherwood** (robertajsherwood.com)
Peter Slater (railshotsuk.com)	**Nick Slocombe** (http://nick86235.smugmug.com)
Jamie Squibbs (jamiesquibbs.com)	**Steve Stubbs**
Mark Thomas (walesrails.smugmug.com)	**Mick Tindall**
John Whitehouse (flickr.com/photos/wulfruna_kid)	**Chris Williams** (flickr.com/photos/chrisjohnw)
Martin Williams	**Michael Wright** (mawrailphotography.zenfolio.com)
James Welham (flickr.com/photos/jameswelham)	**Syd Young** (flickr.com/photos/sydpix)

Technical Stuff

Many readers frequently ask the question - "What criteria / standard do digital images have to meet for inclusion in *'Loco Review?'* There is no standard as such, images are judged on the strength of their own merit, except that JPEG images must be 'high-resolution' (see below). Each image is then processed in 'Adobe Photoshop' to ensure the best possible quality. ie:

Image Mode   : CMYK (**C**yan, **M**agenta, **Y**ellow, **K**ey (ie. Black)) colour conversion.

Image Format   : TIFF

Pixels   : 3,070 (Width) 2,350 (Height)

Document Size : Width   26 cms

                     Height   17 cms

                     Resolution   300 pixels per inch.

Each digital image is checked for colour balance, sharpness and contrast after any cropping and straightening; any glitches and marks are removed using the 'Clone' tool.

As for sharpness, the 'Unsharp Mask' tool is used for greater accuracy.

Scanned images usually need a little bit more work, especially from contrasty films, such as Fujichrome and Kodachrome 64, which tend to produce excessive green and magenta highlights, respectively.

My Personal Favourite

"Seek and ye shall find" .... I could not close this edition without including the image overleaf, which for me encapsulates what railway photography is all about - seeking out new photographic opportunities. With the towering presence of the Tunstead complex dominating the background, Class 66/0 No.66008 exits the 29 yard long Peak Forest Junction Tunnel and crawls into the only clearing available for this shot of 6H22, the 11:55 Tunstead - Hindlow loaded limestone.   **David Hayes**